MODERNIZE YOUR KISSING!
DISCOVER—

♥ THE NEWEST FADS IN FRENCH KISSING.

♥ HOW TO MAKE YOURSELF KISSABLE IN THE EYES OF THE OPPOSITE SEX

♥ WHERE MEN (AND WOMEN) LIKE TO BE KISSED BEST

♥ TIPS FOR MORE INTIMATE KISSES

♥ HOW TO DO TODAY'S TRENDIEST KISSES:
  ♡ THE UPSIDE-DOWN KISS
  ♡ THE LIP-O-SUCTION KISS
  ♡ THE BUTTERFLY KISS
  ♡ THE ROCK KISS
  ♡ THE TROBRIAND ISLANDS KISS

Here's the eagerly awaited revision of the kissing bible featured on *Donahue* and published in more than eighteen foreign countries. Completely revised and updated through a worldwide Internet survey available to 20 million people, *The Art of Kissing* is your key to every aspect of contemporary kissing excitement.

"Get it and expand *your* puckering portfolio."

—*Seventeen*

"You are bound to learn something new about kissing if you read this book."

—*Newton Bee,* Newton, Connecticut

"*The Art of Kissing* goes beyond the valley of French kissing by exploring . . . such advanced exercises as the underwater kiss, the counterkiss and the electric kiss (rub your stockinged feet on the carpet and *whoa*!)."

—*Washington Times*

"Whoever said 'a kiss is just a kiss' didn't get his mitts on *The Art of Kissing* . . . a detailed how-to book . . . this year's handy alternative to chocolates."

—*Elle*

"It's refreshing to think about kissing per se rather than as a prelude to something else."

—*Self*

"If you . . . want to smooch like Rick and Elsa in *Casablanca,* this bussing bible is for you."

—Lowell (Massachusetts) *Sun*

"Some terrific tips on how you can make every kiss as passionate and thrilling as your first."

—*The National Enquirer*

"I advise you to race full speed to your bookstore and pick up a copy of *The Art of Kissing* . . . it could save you emotional problems."

—*Clarion Ledger*
(Jackson, Mississippi)

"*The Art of Kissing* is perhaps the most thorough encyclopedia on swapping slobber ever available . . . Cane covers every kind of kissing imaginable. . . . Whether you're looking to improve your skills or to save your hide after giving a lousy Valentine's Day gift, *The Art of Kissing* is sure to be effective."

—Richardson (Texas) *News*

"The definitive book . . . lighthearted . . . fun . . . worth more than lip service!"

—Oxford (England) *Mail*

The

Art of Kissing

Also by William Cane

The Book of Kisses

The Art of Hugging

The

Art of Kissing

Completely Revised and Updated Edition

William Cane

St. Martin's Griffin
New York

For Carla Mayer Glasser

Back cover author photo copyright © 1995 by Terri
McCarthy.
Illustrations © 1995 by Durell Godfrey.

Library of Congress Cataloging-in-Publication Data

Cane, William.
    The art of kissing / William Cane. —Rev. ed.
      p.   cm.
   ISBN 0-312-11744-2 (pbk.)
   1. Kissing.   I. Title.
  GT2640.C36   1995
  394—dc20   94-39204
                        CIP

10   9   8

CONTENTS

PREFACE TO THE COMPLETELY REVISED AND UPDATED EDITION

One morning as I was getting ready to give my English class a break, Beth, a pert sixteen-year-old student, approached my desk with her vocabulary test in hand.

"I heard you were an expert on kissing."

"Well, I *did* write a book on it, but—"

"Did you ever hear of *this* one?"

She flipped over her test. On the back of it she'd drawn a man and woman with lips locked.

"It's called lip-o-suction."

She started explaining it to me. Suddenly other students were crowded around, listening, throwing in their two cents: "Yeah, sure, I tried that one." "Have you heard about the one where you use your eyelashes?"

Vocabulary was no longer the topic. Within minutes I was surrounded by twenty teenagers who knew more about tongue action than a panel of sexologists. I started to think it was time for this teacher to take a refresher course. On that day, I decided to begin working on a completely revised and updated edition of *The Art of Kissing*.

What's new in this revised edition?

Virtually everything. The book you hold in your hands contains the latest information available on kissing. Each chapter has been revised and brought up to date with new data gathered through a worldwide kissing survey. Which types of kisses do women like most? What tongue techniques will impress your man? You'll find the answers here, as well as new sections on romance, and a chapter on how to make yourself more kissable. There are also new chapters on the upside-down kiss, the butterfly kiss, the friendly kiss, and of course the lip-o-suction kiss. We've added new comments from kissers around the world, and included more precise instructions for most kisses. For example, the chapter on the French kiss has been expanded with information about the latest fads in tongue licking.

Research for this edition was gathered through the first major survey on kissing distributed through the Internet, a computer network of more than 20 million people worldwide. We received thousands of responses from across the country and around the world, with people in nineteen foreign countries responding.

If you'd like to be on the mailing list for future revisions, send a business-size self-addressed, stamped envelope to me at P.O. Box 1422, Brookline, MA 02146-0011 or send e-mail to mike@kissing.com and feel free to include any comments or suggestions about kissing. Remember that all responses will remain anonymous and that by sending your comments you agree that they may be used anonymously in future editions of this book.

You can also contribute your thoughts on kissing, hugging, and relationships to my next book by visiting the unofficial *The Art of Kissing* homepage on the World-Wide Web at http://www.kissing.com/aok.html.

Kiss them well.

William Cane
Jaunuary 1995

$\mathcal{P}$REFACE

This book is the result of a kiss, and a rather embarrassing one at that. I had been kissing a certain young woman when she broke off and pushed away, her mouth a gaping oval of surprise and her blue eyes wide with shock and annoyance. I was taken aback by this sudden reversal of emotion: A moment before she had been kissing me passionately.

"You're not supposed to kiss with your eyes open," she said.

I was totally bewildered. Where in the book of kissing did it say that you had to kiss with your eyes closed? I asked her, but she couldn't tell me. "It's not nice to kiss and look," she insisted. And because she liked to kiss with her eyes closed I had to follow suit. That was her logic, and of course—being under her spell—I played by her rules.

But I was vexed, for I wanted to be able to refer to some authority to show that it was all right to kiss with your eyes open. Unfortunately the books on kissing that I consulted at the library were woefully silent on this and many other points. The best of the old books, *The Art of Kissing,* by Hugh Morris (1936), discussed a number of kisses in separate chapters, but its treatment was out-of-date and often consisted of merely a collection of quotes from classical poets. Neither Morris nor the other writers gave more than a perfunctory description of how to execute the kisses they discussed. It was as if they avoided detail on purpose.

Puzzled at the lack of explicitness in these works, I set out to obtain the information myself. Over a period of ten years I gathered most of the data in this book through interviews and the first worldwide Internet survey on kissing.

Part One examines the psychology of kissing, dealing with emotional and sensual features and placing the subject in context. Part Two (The Kissing Encyclopedia) and Part Three (Kisses from Around the World) describe and explain in separate chapters how to execute familiar classics as well as the most exotic new kisses. Part Four examines almost every conceivable aspect of kissing technique, summarizing current practices, pinpointing what men and women like and don't like, and letting you benefit from the experiences of your contemporaries.

In addition to the thousands of people around the world who answered the Internet kissing survey, and many others too numerous to mention here, I'm thankful for the help and encouragement I received from my parents, my sister, my brothers, Rhea Becker, Mark A. Fischer, Cathy Foley, and my agent, Carla Mayer Glasser. I'm especially indebted to Terri McCarthy for her creative advice on the Internet questionnaire.

PART ONE

The Psychology of Kissing

WHAT IS KISSING?

Everyone knows what a kiss is. If we had to be blunt and direct, we could agree with Dr. Henry Gibbons that a kiss is simply "the anatomical juxtaposition of two *orbicularis oris* muscles in a state of contraction." But who wants to be blunt and direct? The real point is, What does kissing mean? What does it do to you? How does it make you feel? To answer those questions, you have to ask people who are in love or who are infatuated, because they—and not dictionaries—are the true experts when it comes to defining what kissing is.

What do you like most about kissing?

WOMEN:
"I just love to kiss. It's the biggest turn-on."

"I like the feeling of breathing someone else's space, sharing with them the basis of life, i.e., air. There's that inexplicable feeling that's like having an extreme, uncontrollable case of the shivers, but not quite, and being so close to someone that you can really smell what their scent is."

"It lowers my blood pressure, warms my mood, and

suppresses my appetite for sweet things, especially choc- olate. I feel intoxicated (only with the right guy) and want to kiss for a long time. It's not necessarily a prelude to sex. It's a spiritual connection, exploring and devouring. Some- times it makes me shake, sweat, laugh uncontrollably."

"Being held close while it is happening—like I am a fragile, precious thing."

"The thing I like most about kissing is the closeness it creates. Also you can tell a lot from a kiss. A kiss is like a window into someone's inner thoughts. You can sense the mood of the person you're kissing. You can often tell how they really feel about you from a kiss. Someone who really cares for you will not kiss you the same way as someone who is just there for sex. Another thing I like about kissing is that it always foreshadows what might be coming."

"Being able to vary it so much—French kiss, regular kiss, on the side of the mouth, biting, licking, sucking, exploring. It's never boring! And you have your hands free to touch other parts, too."

"Sexually, it's expressive . . . exciting . . . usually the first tactile contact you have with the other person. It's warming and brings you close. Nonsexually, it's affec- tionate, friendly."

"I like being physically close to the other person . . . the closeness, hugging, and arms intertwined, more than the actual kiss, except in unusual cases."

MEN:
"I like a violent and slightly wet mouth."

"My girlfriend's breath, the feel of her lips and tongue."

"I can't quite put my finger on it, whether it's the hunger of passion, some mystical unknown sense developed in my mouth, the soft cat-showers and massages, or being in contact with my woman's sexy mouth or legs. I'm so overwhelmed by the experience, the feelings are not simple, and they saturate my mind with pleasure."

Is there anything you don't like about kissing?

WOMEN:
"Smoker's breath!"

"Beard burn; bad breath; when it doesn't vary at all."

"When a person isn't gentle or sensual: too deep and passionate a kiss before I'm ready for it. When a person glosses over kissing just to get to the next step."

"Being kissed with an open mouth when you only *like* the kisser."

"When people I don't know kiss me on the mouth. My brother-in-law kisses with his tongue out. Everybody hates to kiss him."

"Sometimes a man with no subtlety will thrust a pasty tongue into your mouth and it's like *oral rape!* A misfit of mouths. Or a man who has no passion in kissing. A too-delicate kisser can be irritating."

Do you ever get very aroused simply by kissing?

WOMEN:
"Definitely! It makes my mouth tingle, my head gets dizzy, and my blood runs hotter through my veins."

"Yes, yes, yes, yes. I have a one-and-a-half-year friendship that includes only kissing and petting, and *boy* do I get aroused. It's amazing. Especially since I know it won't go further, it's also tantalizing."

"Arousal starts with the kiss for me. Okay, maybe it starts before that. But the kiss most definitely gets me moving along."

"Yes, if we're standing very close to each other."

"Yes. When kisses are very slow, gentle, wet, accompanied by light touches to the face and neck."

MEN:
"Positively yes."

"Ever? Always."

"Very. It's as close as you can get to anyone before it gets obscene in public. If you're Frenching, it's like giving yourself to one another."

"Yes. For example, a prolonged surprise kiss in the kitchen once led to kissing and cuddling on the living-room floor."

What goes through your mind when you kiss?

WOMEN:
"Generally it's the physical sensations I'm aware of. Mentally I'm evaluating the kissing ability of the other person, the give-and-take and the response of the other person."

"How's he feeling? Does he really care for me? Does he like the *way* I kiss? What's going to happen if we both get out of control?"

"I like to see how turned on he gets. Usually it's as much as I do."

"It's about time he kissed me!"

MEN:

"I'm thinking about the kiss itself: 'Am I enjoying it? *What* am I enjoying about it? What am I going to do in return?' If I'm *not* enjoying it, *that's* what I'm thinking about."

"I daydream about what she would be like if she were naked in bed. Sometimes I wonder what it would be like to be married to the person."

"What a lucky thrill I'm getting!"

"I often wonder what's next. Your mind immediately starts to think about sex and intercourse."

"A warm, relaxed feeling."

"How far I'll get with the girl."

Of course it's easiest to get some perspective on kissing by asking people about it directly, but for a truly comprehensive analysis we've got to make a brief detour into the realm of zoology. It's an incontrovertible fact that animals kiss, too. When anthropologist Jane Goodall studied chimpanzees at the Gombe National Park in Tanzania, Africa, she discovered that they kissed for a variety of different reasons and in a number of different social contexts. Some chimps kissed as a submissive gesture. They also kissed when greeting chimps they knew, or for what we would consider romantic reasons, such as when developing a relationship.

Comparatively speaking, chimpanzee kisses are probably closest to human kisses, but many other species of animals also kiss, including horses during courtship, dogs during play, and even some fishes. Kissing fishes will often swim around with their lips locked to another fish's lips for hours in an exhibition of kissing stamina that few humans can match. Throughout the animal kingdom, then, kissing expresses tender emotions as well as strong sexual desire. But as for what's going through the mind of those fishes . . . your guess is as good as mine.

Next time you're with your lover, start a conversation about how animals kiss. When you're trying to break the ice, describe a few kissing chimps or fishes for your partner, and I guarantee that it won't be long before the two of you are enjoying a few kisses of your own.

LET'S GET ROMANTIC

One young woman wrote to me about the day she went with her boyfriend to a huge festival. A sudden cloudburst forced them to run to a table with an umbrella on it. Quickly they jumped up on the table and pulled the umbrella down around themselves a little. They were dripping wet, watching all of the people running around. But they had found their own little spot! Her boyfriend leaned close and kissed her. They were right in front of a wine booth. Eventually one of the men working at the booth ran out in the pouring rain with a glass of wine for each of them. They both felt so wonderful. For the next forty-five minutes they sat there holding each other, kissing, and drinking wine in their own secluded world.

This is romantic kissing! When you can create your own private world with just you and your lover, kissing can be the focus of what feels like an eternity of pleasure. The key is to create—or find by luck—an element of romance wherever you are. And the key to romance, according to survey replies, seems to be a kind of isolation where you and your lover can be alone together away from your day-to-day concerns.

A nineteen-year-old from Hawaii had his most romantic kiss on a live volcano. He took his girlfriend out to the shelf where lava rolled into the ocean, shrieking with steam and heat every time a wave came in, now and then surging and making deep low explosions underground. Bathed in an eerie orange glow, they stood on the edge of land no more than two weeks old. It was three A.M., but hot enough to be noon in the summer. The young man turned to his girlfriend and said, "I really would take you to the ends of the earth for even a single kiss." For the next ten minutes they smooched by the light of the sheer power of nature melting rocks.

When I asked people to describe the most romantic places they ever kissed, their answers almost always referred to this type of ends-of-the-earth isolation. They mentioned an apple orchard, a beach, being in a glass elevator, out in a field looking at the stars, at a beaver pond in a secluded area, on top of the Eiffel Tower in France, or on a train ride together.

That special togetherness is evident in this reply from a twenty-four-year-old woman from New York City:

"My most romantic kiss was atop the Empire State Building. My boyfriend and I had just carved our initials and a heart into the windowsill of one of the observatory windows. Then he told me to put my hand over it. He put his hand on mine, we kissed, and he said, 'And now that'll keep that there forever.' "

Those who enjoyed these kinds of romantic kisses often felt kissing was more intimate than sex. In fact when I asked "What do you think is more intimate, kissing or sex?" 50 percent of men and 75 percent of women said kissing.

What do you think is more intimate, kissing or sex?
WOMEN:
"I think that kissing is more intimate, because I've found that if I'm having sex with someone that I don't find too

interesting personality-wise, then I don't want to kiss them at all. But if I'm romantically involved and really enjoy the person that I'm with, then I want to kiss them for hours."

"My boyfriend (of three years) and I have been discussing this question ad nauseam lately and, frankly, I think kissing is much more intimate than having sex. Kissing is such a connection! I mean, it's nearly impossible to kiss someone and not stay physically and mentally involved. Sometimes we surprise each other if we get more aroused and excited about each other by just kissing as opposed to having sex."

MEN:
"When we're talking about real good kissing, kissing is more intimate."

"Kissing, except if sex is damn good with a person I love."

Does kissing always have to lead to other sexual acts?
WOMEN:
"No, no, a thousand times NO! Kissing in and of itself is wonderful and should not be taken for granted. My lover and I often sit for hours and kiss and touch and cuddle with each other without anything else happening and no clothes being removed (except shoes)."

"I love kissing for the sake of kissing. To me, kissing and sex are two very different and separate activities."

"Many men think kisses always should lead to intercourse, so I usually don't get *too* involved with kissing unless I want to end up making love."

"Kissing by itself can be very sensual and sexy and is not just part of a ritual before sex."

The opinions of these young women represent a bold new way of looking at the sensual aspects of kissing. They're suggesting that kissing can stand alone as a sensual pleasure that deserves to be enjoyed for itself without going on to other sex acts. Kissing can bring two people closer than ******** because it's a more personal interaction. Which is why many prostitutes won't kiss their customers. "I don't kiss my customers," said one prostitute during a recent Cinemax interview. "That's too personal of a thing." They'll ******** for hours but won't kiss because kissing is considered even more intimate than ********!

The past few years have witnessed a groundswell of new interest in kissing as a contemporary generation of lovers redefines what it considers romantic. Recent sex surveys indicate that modern lovers believe kissing is one of the most essential aspects of a relationship, yet men and women are increasingly reporting that there is not enough kissing in their love lives. For example, a recent survey of

---

Kissing Tip

The following romantic things are often cited by men and women as getting them in the mood to kiss: taking a stroll through a park or along a quiet street; holding hands; romantic (not adult!) movies; music; intelligent open conversation; poetry; back-rubs; fireworks; roses; dim lights; cuddling; physical closeness; candlelight; nice scenery; twilight. In addition, most men mentioned: the smell of good perfume; those kissable lips; a sexy outfit; looking at the opposite sex and getting turned on; and flirting.

more than 4,000 men showed that of all foreplay activities kissing was considered the most enjoyable. At the same time another survey—*The Hite Report on Male Sexuality*—indicated that many men want more kissing in their relationships. And *The Hite Report* itself, just like the women quoted in this chapter, revealed that many women rated the pleasure they received from kissing higher than the pleasure they received from any other type of sexual activity, yet they frequently complained that there wasn't enough kissing in their love lives. Lovers take note: There is a growing interest on the part of women and men in the nongenital aspects of sexual intimacy, including kissing, all of which suggests that kissing is perhaps the most sensuous form of loveplay. Indeed, a lot of people like it so much that they seem to think that they are somehow alone in their insatiable desire to kiss. Many people told me confidently: "I like to kiss more than just about anybody!"

How to make your-self more kissable

"Ooooooooooooooh!" Jessica was saying to her friend Nicole. "Look! Look! Look!" The two attractive teenagers were standing outside their university's cafeteria on a sunny afternoon.

"What is it?"

"Check out that guy!"

"Which one?"

"The one with the mustache. Oooooooooooooh! Help me! Help me! Help me!"

"What's wrong?"

"I'm dying to kiss him. Can't you tell? He's gorgeous! Oh, please, God, I'm going to faint if he comes over here."

"Don't look now, but he's headed this way."

"I'm so in love with him—and with that mouth! I want to kiss him to death I'm so crazy about him."

This is an actual conversation I overheard recently at a large university. It started me wondering how some people manage to project such a highly kissable image. What is it, I asked men and women, that makes you want to kiss a member of the opposite sex? The results were nearly unanimous: good looks, a winning smile, a positive mental attitude, fresh breath, and beautiful lips and teeth.

Are you kissable?

1. Do you dress fashionably?
2. Do you keep your hair neat?
3. Have you ever asked a member of the opposite sex for advice on how to look sexier?
4. Do you have a positive mental attitude?
5. Do you frequently smile?
6. Is your breath fresh?

The more YES answers, the higher your kissability score.

How do you keep your breath fresh for kissing?

MEN:

"Breath mints, mouthwash, a minty toothpaste. More breath mints. More breath mints. More breath mints."

"Gum works, but I hate that chewing. A tiny breath mint is fine!"

"For early morning kisses, I have been known to have a small glass of mouthwash on the nightstand. Depends on how light a sleeper she is and on whether you can use the mouthwash without making it *sound* like you're using it."

"Brushing teeth just before kissing, or, if I don't have the chance to beforehand, staying away from malodorous foods as much as possible."

WOMEN:

"I'm a vegetarian (according to an old boyfriend it makes a difference), I brush and floss every day, and if I'm planning on kissing someone I tend to eat the same sorts of things they do at dinner."

"Don't drink coffee. Eat fruit and vegetables."

"Sometimes I use chocolate to make my mouth taste really sweet."

"Breath mints . . . or prayer."

Kissing Tip

Here's what dental hygienists recommend for fresh breath, in descending order of importance:

- Floss and brush your teeth.
- Brush your tongue (yes, *tongue!*) to remove bacteria.
- Drink plenty of water to wash away odor-producing bacteria.
- Use antimicrobial mouthwashes (although their effect lasts only about one hour).
- Use breath mints and sprays only as a *last resort* since they merely *mask* odor and don't remove it.
- Maintain a low-fat, high-carbohydrate diet, which will tend to sweeten your breath.

How do you project a kissable image for the opposite sex?

MEN:
"First and foremost, smile! Try to keep neatly shaven. Talk with your eyes—hold their gaze intently."

"Moist lips and occasional licking of the lips. Occasional biting of the upper lip."

"Just by being me. (Damn, that sounds conceited.) But it's true. I'm an attractive fellow and have a great personality. I get kissed for being me."

"By having a tidy, clean appearance. And by finding out what a particular woman likes to see in someone before kissing them. In the present case, this means wearing my hair long and dressing simply."

WOMEN:
"I use my hair and *that look*. Works every time."

"I smile a lot, and I tend to give goodbye kisses pretty easily (hugs, too) so I get more serious kisses."

"I make sure to always wear a muted, soft lipstick."

"Try to keep eye contact while talking because their peripheral vision picks up your mouth moving and then they can't help but keep looking at your mouth."

Do you have any tips on how to make the lips and teeth irresistible?

MEN:
"Put Vaseline on in the evening before bed."

"When brushing your teeth, run the toothbrush over your lips as well, as this removes all those little bits of skin that crop up."

WOMEN:
"I find that occasionally pursing my lips, or pressing my lips together, will cause a man to think about kissing me. Also, running your tongue around your lips works wonders!"

"Don't use Chapstick! Waxy lips are really yucky."

"I use just clear gloss now, because lipstick seems to keep him from kissing me."

"I like putting Vaseline or something slippery on my lips."

"As far as lips go, I'm a lip balm addict and don't go *anywhere* without it. But anything with menthol–smelling stuff in it . . . *stay away!* Also, brushing your lips *gently* with a damp toothbrush once a week helps, especially in the winter."

"If I knew how to make my teeth and lips irresistible, I would not be here right now completing this survey, I would be home kissing someone."

What specific things (either physical or emotional) make you want to kiss someone of the opposite sex?

MEN:
"It's a combination of things. Serious kisses come after considerable preparations have been made, like lighting, music, food, location, and mood. That's when thick, full, tender kisses are the best."

"Good looks. Nice smell (I prefer natural smells to perfume), girls who are *up* and *fun*. Girls who aren't too short (I'm a basketball player). Long hair."

"Similar educational and moral background. Long hair. *Wanting* eyes."

"It's always a pleasurable experience to gaze into the eyes when speaking to a woman. But I find it very hard to do this, since I'm strongly attracted to a woman's mouth. Sometimes I catch myself watching her talk or staring at her earrings."

WOMEN:

"When men have really full lips—I love full lips!—or if they're wearing a ripped T-shirt or something . . . their eyes, too. They have to look very sultry."

"Someone who smiles a lot, who is open to hugs and cuddles, who gets signals that I'm interested, who has lots of intelligent things coming out between those lips."

"First and foremost, their brain. You may be initially attracted to someone by physical appearance, but that usually wears off in about five minutes. I've met many people whose looks left something to be desired, but after talking to them for about half an hour, all I wanted to do was jump them. Long dark hair and intense eyes of any color don't hurt. And the taller the better."

"I have a specific lip shape that appeals to me. But more important, I have to know they are interested. I can't just kiss for the sake of kissing, say at the end of a date because it's expected."

"Physical traits may cause me to think/hope/fantasize about kissing a man. However, I'll feel moved to do so only if I know him well, have fallen for his personality, and sense that this feeling is mutual. I'm sort of a fuddy-duddy when it comes to relationships and kissing. I've never kissed a stranger or an acquaintance—never wanted to. To me, kissing is an investment in itself, and just because a person is attractive doesn't mean a kiss will occur. Basically, my heart must be won over."

Mustaches, beards, stubble

Women are almost evenly divided on whether they like kissing guys with mustaches and beards. Slightly more (53 percent) say they like a clean-shaven face, while 40 percent like a mustache or beard, and 7 percent say it doesn't matter to them.

Stubble is less popular. But although most women (two out of three) don't like kissing guys with stubble, one in three says it's a distinct turn-on. Said one thirty-year-old woman, "I love it when he doesn't shave for a day or two; he starts looking like a cowboy and I just want to ride away with him."

Advice for men

Once in a while try showing up for a date without shaving. Then ask if she likes kissing you like that. You might be pleasantly surprised.

WOMEN ON MUSTACHES, BEARDS, AND STUBBLE:
"I don't like kissing guys with *just* mustaches. If it's attached to a beard, yes. Mustaches on their own look like caterpillars on men's faces. But beards seem to make a man's lips seem more luscious. They feel nice when they're nuzzling your neck, too."

"What I *do* like in facial hair is stubble . . . about two days' worth. It's not so much aesthetically pleasing as it is fun to feel on your face."

"I like kissing! As long as there isn't a lot of sandpaper-stubble, I don't mind facial hair of any kind! Actually, kissing a man with a beard can be ticklish!"

Lipstick

Most women worry about whether men will mind kissing them with it on. Here's what men had to say.

MEN ON LIPSTICK:
"I don't mind, provided the lipstick *tastes* good."

"Not at all. In fact, I *like* those lipsticks that have flavor to them."

"I don't mind unless it is scented/flavored. I don't care for that."

"Variety is the key to wearing lipstick. The idea that one and only one color is *right* for you is a myth propagated by the cosmetics industry. Some women wear the same color every day. How would you like it if your boyfriend wore the same orange shirt every day? I love it when a woman varies things—sometimes wearing no lipstick for a natural sisterly look that can be supremely sexy, other times wearing a blood-red, nasty-girl color or switching to a hot pink or flesh-colored tone, sometimes wearing a matte look, other times a glossy look. I love it all! Just give me some variety, not the *same blood-red* every day. And do you know what can be really sexy sometimes—white or ivory-colored lipstick! Be adventurous! Check out the pale lipstick on the dancers in the Rod Stewart video *This Old Heart of Mine*. Wow!"

"I love coming home from a date with lipstick stains on my shirt and face. It's so romantic it makes me feel like I'm in a movie!"

Advice for women

During kissing, most men (67 percent) *don't mind* if you wear lipstick, and 8 percent actually like it when you wear *flavored* lipstick. A minority of men (25 percent) won't enjoy kissing you if you're wearing lipstick, usually because of the smell or taste.

Sure, you can work to improve your kissability, but *should* you? As one thirty-year-old woman from Leeds, England, summed it up, "I don't think you need to project a kissable image. They'll just want to do it anyway." Probably no truer testament to the irrepressible drive to kiss was ever uttered! Oh, where would we be without that wonderful, wonderful kick in the seat of the pants, that jolt to the nervous system that gets us running after members of the opposite sex and wanting to kiss * kiss * kiss * kiss * kiss * kiss * kiss? But then again if you *just happen* to know a few tricks of the trade, can it really hurt?

PART TWO

The
Kissing
Encyclopedia

The
$\mathcal{F}$IRST KISS

Not surprisingly, most people can remember their first kiss; whether it happened ten or fifty years ago, it seemed to have left an indelible impression on them.

Do you remember your first kiss?

Can remember	93%
Can't remember	7%

WOMEN:
"This is one of my favorite stories. I was very attracted to the boy involved, and we had been having shy flirtatious conversations for some time. One day we were sitting together and talking, and suddenly he looked me straight in the eye and said, 'May I give you a kiss?' After controlling my panic I squeaked, 'Yes, you may.' He then got up and got a bag of Hershey's kisses and gave me one! I blushed a lot, we both laughed, and he said he'd hoped I'd fall for that. Then after a few more shy looks he gave me the other kind of kiss."

"My first kiss with G— was in my room. I was seventeen years old. We were listening to music, and the moment was right. We leaned toward each other, and I knew we were about to kiss. In anticipation I shut my eyes and puckered up, ready for my lips to meet his. They never did . . . he had his mouth *open* instead of puckered, so instead of meeting his lips, I met his tonsils! When I suddenly felt this big wet mouth encompassing my face (no joke, he got my nose, my chin . . .), I burst into hysterical laughter. My first kiss with G- started out so romantically, and ended up with me curled up on the floor giggling!''

"Talk about stressful! The boy and I froze in place after discussing the inevitability of the kiss happening for at least half an hour. With that kind of buildup it was impossible to enjoy it."

"My heart exploded. I was one happy rubber-chested gal the next day. A New Year's party. I was fourteen or fifteen. His name was Gary, a boy my age, a schoolmate. My first experience drinking hard liquor (or any kind of liquor). I let him touch my breasts under my shirt. We kissed for hours on a couch in a den of a friend's house. Then he drove me to a place where we watched planes take off from the airport, soaring, blasting close overhead. More kissing. More thrill to the bone marrow. I still remember his breath, and occasionally the scent comes back to me."

"I was twelve. He was a fourteen-year-old guy who was in a play with me in junior high. We had the two lead parts, and we fell in love. It was opening night of the play and we were waiting backstage. The play was a Western and I was a saloon girl, so I had bright lipstick on. One of the guys who used to flirt with me said, 'Madam, let me take that lipstick off your face,' then attempted to kiss me. Instead, Tom (my boyfriend-to-be) stepped in and said, 'No, let me do it.' He took me in his arms, leaned me back Hollywood style, and gave me a long, slow French kiss. I was thrilled and excited. The play went great! The next day I felt more mature and definitely happy."

"When Ray and I first met we were in high school. He was a senior and I a junior. I fell in love with him at first sight and said to myself that he would someday be my husband. Five years later my dream came true. We were best friends and still are, I'll never forget the first time we kissed. I was tired of chasing him. He kept telling his friends that he didn't like me, but his friends wanted us to be together, and they told me that he liked me so I kept talking to him. Then I got frustrated trying to figure out what the heck he wanted and I left him alone. I actually got a bit irritated with him.

"It was the last day of school before Christmas vacation. We used to walk down a seldom-used stairwell together and on this particular day, because everyone had rushed out of school for vacation, the halls were unusually vacant. He and I were walking down the steps together and he sensed my irritation with him. He asked me what was wrong and instead of saying that I was upset because of his behavior and my confusion, I stopped on the step lower than him, looked him square in the face, eyes locked, and I planted one on him. It seemed to suspend us in time and I felt as though I had never kissed another before. It literally took my breath away, and although I had never made love to anyone, I felt this was my first time, especially since I became so excited I even reached climax.

"Nothing touched except our lips, but the moment just swept us away and we became one. Making love in the literal sense came later on, much later. But I felt then, as I do now, that that kiss defined lovemaking for me. It happened over ten years ago but I can still feel that kiss—his shocked look at first and then the total giving on the part of each of us. It was as if we knocked down all barriers and it was all right to admit that we loved each other."

MEN:

"I was fourteen years old, and I kissed a girl I had a crush on named Karen. It felt great, though she was eight inches taller than I was. I felt like I was floating on a cloud. I was a little embarrassed because she kissed me in front of my whole soccer team."

"Surprising. Didn't see it coming. I was on a Ferris wheel at the time, and wasn't sure if the funny feeling in my stomach was attraction or vertigo."

"My first kiss was incredible. I was fourteen and we were playing truth-or-dare at a party, and someone dared me to French-kiss a girl that I (and every other guy in my school) wanted very badly. She was an extremely attractive girl with a fantastic mouth. I had no emotional connection with her, but the kiss was fantastic, and she also seemed to be pleased. That thrill will follow me for the rest of my days."

"FIRE, FIRE, FIRE! Man it was wonderful! It melted me."

"A disaster. (What should I do with my tongue?)"

> ### Kissing Tip
>
> Even if you're an experienced lover whose first kiss occurred many years ago, remember there's always that first romantic kiss with someone new.

How to overcome shyness

Some people like to savor the shyness of the first kiss. It gives them an all-choked-up-inside feeling, and for them the initial shyness is what makes the first kiss so memorable. But excessive shyness can hinder your enjoyment. Here's how to reduce your first-kiss jitters:

1. Arrange to have that first kiss in a fun or playful context. About 5 percent of people experienced their first kiss while playing a kissing game. Kissing under mistletoe is another example of using a nonthreatening situation to get things started.

2. Get close enough to the other person so that your feelings take control. The key is to get within kissing distance, which is about one foot away from him—so close that you can feel his body heat. This is why lovers often make believe they see something in their partner's eye. Anything to get him close will usually do the trick. If you're both ready for the kiss and you get close enough, it happens automatically.

3. It's generally not a good idea to *ask* for a kiss. It's much better to say something like, "I'd like to kiss you." Sometimes it's even appropriate to make a demand. Remember Shakespeare's line from *The Taming of the Shrew*: "Kiss me, Kate!" You can start the ball rolling with the same line. Said one young woman: "One time I told a boy I was dating that if he didn't kiss me soon—we would *stop* dating."

4. For a more subtle approach, catch your partner's eye when you're out together. Most men say they take their cue about kissing from the woman, usually from observing her behavior toward them. If she stands close, smiles warmly, holds eye contact, and generally looks like she wants to be kissed, then the man feels encouraged to initiate the kiss. You can often tell if a man wants to kiss you by looking at his eyes; if he's staring at your mouth he's ready to kiss you. After you've gone on a few dates, watch him closely when you're saying

good night. When you see him staring at your mouth, stop whatever you're doing and look dreamily at him. Usually he'll take the hint and kiss you.

What advice can you give to a shy person?

"Shyness can be good in kissing, but you also have to know when to ask if you're doing something right. I'm a former shy person and I *know* this is difficult, but if you're kissing the right person, it should be okay. Not to mention everyone should have some degree of faith in their natural ability."

"Well, it is a pretty intimate thing to be doing. If you don't feel comfortable, start slowly. You don't have to initiate kisses if you're really shy about it, but if you get used to giving pecks hello and goodbye with your friends 'real' kissing seems to come more naturally."

"Try holding hands and nuzzling for a while, the kiss will come on eventually. Get physically comfortable with the other person first."

"Relax and enjoy. There's no correct way to kiss, so don't worry about doing anything wrong."

"Let loose and don't worry about what you look like up close; usually the other person's eyes are closed."

"Start slow and gradually let yourself go; loosen up."

"Relax and don't be uptight—it'll happen. If you think too much you might just screw it up."

How to make all your kisses feel like first kisses

The secret of erotic kissing is to make each and every kiss feel like a first. Here's how to recapture the thrill that usually accompanies a first kiss:

1. Think of your lover as a stranger and imagine that you're meeting for the first time. Many men and women said they used this technique successfully.
2. It sometimes helps to go to new places, new settings, because this acts as a spur to the imagination.
3. Give your partner a teasing kiss. Many people who have been kissing for years get too serious about their kisses, and a teasing kiss can lighten things up.
4. Don't anticipate. Sometimes lovers get into a rut, anticipating what will happen next, looking forward to the usual patterns that their lovemaking takes. In order to break out of this rut, tell yourself that you're *not* going to go on in your usual way, that you're simply going to dally and play for a while.
5. Try an upside-down kiss—from that angle your lover will actually *look* like a different person.

The first kiss can be attempted and successfully executed in a number of ways. The most popular way is to get to know the person and then get physically close. For those who have been kissing for years and who thought it was all downhill from here—it isn't! By following some of the suggestions given above, you can experience the wonder of the first kiss all over again. Stage actors face this challenge each time they have to play a scene before a new audience. Alas, your audience may not always be new, but your kissing can be if you concentrate on the experience.

The
$\mathcal{L}$IP KISS

"Sometimes when I look at a stranger's lips close up and they look quite kissable, I think, 'Oh, I would like to kiss those lips!' " In saying so, didn't this twenty-five-year-old woman voice a feeling common to all lovers? In fact, both men and women have told me that they regularly daydream about lips. A moist red bow parted over a set of even white teeth . . . Ah, it's a natural invitation to kiss! Which is why all lovers should keep their lips kissable: If your lips are cute and moist they'll draw others toward you with irresistible allure.

Sure, the lip kiss is the most basic kiss, and you do it by simply puckering up, moving close, and pressing your lips to your lover's. But such a description is only the beginning of the story. Said one young woman: "I enjoy the *creativity* behind kissing—the many combinations possible using the lips." *The many combinations!* This is the key. And yet all you really need to know to get started is how to approach, what to do during the kiss, and how to break off.

How to approach

Imagine that your lover's lips are pressed together in a demure red bow. Try simply touching your closed lips to the lips of your lover. What passion such a simple initial encounter can generate! You hold back and remain lethargic, not opening your lips the slightest, simply touching them lightly to your lover's. That simple contact will be enough to excite you both to the core, and you'll feel the blood beating in each other's lips.

Another approach is to move in carefully so that you make contact with only your lover's lower lip. As soon as you make contact, stop and simply settle into the kiss slowly and softly, savoring the warmth of your lover's flesh.

Initial lip contact can also be made rather haphazardly, slowly, almost hypnotically as the result of prolonged eye contact. After you've been talking with a lover for a long time, if you've been sitting close and looking into each other's eyes, you'll feel a tension mounting between you that almost draws the two of you together. Let this tension build, and as your faces get close don't worry if your noses bump; simply tilt your head slightly and press onward until your lips touch.

As one young woman explained, "I have on impulse leaned over and kissed someone while they were talking to me sitting on a couch. They seemed pleased when I did, so I might try it again." A thirty-year-old fellow from Ontario, Canada, likes to hug his partner, nuzzling her cheek for a while. Then he goes for the lips. "But sometimes she isn't in the mood for lip kisses," he says, and if that's the case he kisses her cheek for a while.

What to do during the kiss

Unfortunately even in this revolutionary age some people are still skittish about kissing. Once they make lip contact they seem to be in a rush to break off. They may unconsciously think that lip contact is dirty or nasty or prohibited, and these ideas may make them afraid of longer kisses. Such myths interfere with real enjoyment. You've got to learn to settle down, relax, and enjoy the lip kiss. "During a kiss I think about the feel of my partner's lips," said one woman. "I think about the positions of our bodies." Move your limbs into various comfortable positions. Keep in mind that horses will stand together necking for hours, and try to achieve this same animal delight in closeness.

What do you do with your lips and head during a kiss?

WOMAN:
"As far as my lips go, I tend to start slowly with some pressing kisses before going for the open-mouth thing. And I try *desperately* not to give fish kisses, you know, where it feels like the person is gasping for air rather than kissing you? I think people with large mouths are more prone to that."

"I like *still* kissing sometimes, where we just hold our lips together without moving our heads."

"I relax and stay open to whatever might evolve. With some people a very soft feathery long peck feels right, with others more pressure and breaks seem right."

"My head really just moves my lips where I want them to be, but you can do many things with your lips like massage the other's, or suck on the other's, or just touch the other's."

How to break off

There comes a point during every kiss when you've had enough. Some people fear that they might insult their partner by breaking off, and as a result they let a worn-out kiss go on forever. If you're enjoying a really long kiss, all well and good. But when the time comes, you've got to know how to break off. Don't just rip your mouth away unless you want to alarm your lover. Slowly close your lips while they're still in contact with your partner, and pause. Notice whether your partner is initiating another kiss. If your partner is starting another kiss, then you must decide whether you still want to break off. If so, keep your lips closed and pull back gently.

How do you break off from a kiss?

"Either by talking briefly (I like conversation during such moments—something about noise deprivation, perhaps) or by slowing down to a beginning pace."

"Get off my toes, take a breath, move away from their lips to kiss somewhere else. My favorite technique is to break the lip contact and rub noses, Eskimo style."

"Close your mouth more and more and pull away."

"Slowly, lightly, so she doesn't know when I've stopped kissing her."

The
Eye Kiss

You're kissing your boyfriend, let's say, when you happen to open your eyes and notice that he's got a very sweet expression on his face. He's also got his eyes closed. You've been kissing his lips, but the way he looks with his lashes demurely down gives you ideas so that you begin to kiss him on his cheek at the side of the mouth, and then little by little, giving him a series of rather quick kisses as you go, you begin to travel up the side of his face to his eyes, where you softly place the lightest, most tender kisses you can deliver, first on one eye and then on the other.

For such an unusual kiss, a surprising 75 percent of women and 67 percent of men said they liked it. Because the eye kiss has tender and romantic connotations, it occasionally appears in love stories. In chapter six of Hemingway's *A Farewell to Arms,* Frederic kisses his lover with some eye kisses. First he gives her a regular kiss, almost to pave the way for the eye kiss. Then when he sees that her eyes are shut, he kisses both her shut eyes.

Tips for kissing the eyes

- Start with other kisses to lull your partner into a relaxed and receptive state.
- When your partner closes his or her eyes, kiss one shut eye gently, then the other.
- Return often to the lips to keep your partner satisfied. Think of eye kisses as a novelty, a diversion.
- If your partner is wearing contacts, be extra careful.

Do you wear glasses or did you ever kiss someone who did? If so, what advice can you offer on how to kiss someone who wears glasses?

WOMEN:

"I don't wear glasses on a regular basis, but for some reason I'm *insanely* attracted to men in specs. If someone wears glasses, usually they'll stop after the first minute of kissing to remove them because they get fogged up. Or it's always fun after the first couple of kisses to stop yourself, pull back a bit, take them off the person, and say something like, 'We don't want anything to get in the way, do we?' "

"I do wear glasses and experience has shown that two people wearing glasses cannot kiss unless at least one of them takes their glasses off. Better that both remove them if you're planning on kissing for a longer time."

"I wear glasses. I usually have my contacts in, so it's not a problem, but I would suggest that you either take the glasses off—which can be sexy if the other person takes them off and looks or stares into your eyes—or just tilt your head more and be careful and conscious, or don't get so incredibly close to the person."

"I wear glasses and one of my partners wears glasses. I've never had a problem getting tangled up in them, but if I'm really involved in kissing, I tend to take them off."

"I sometimes wear glasses. It's not much of a problem if only one person is wearing them. I say keep 'em on until they get in the way. No use taking 'em off before you ever get kissed . . . looks too desperate!"

"When my partner takes off his glasses, and then mine— I know I'm in for a serious kiss. Other than that, keeping a good sense of humor works well for those times that glasses are in the way."

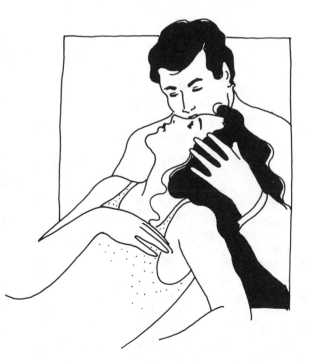

The
EAR KISS

"Every time I kiss her ears she goes wild," one young man from California writes. "It's her most sensitive spot, and I'm sure glad I found it!" His experience is in line with the latest kissing survey, which reveals that 94 percent of women and 87 percent of men enjoy being kissed on their ears. For some, it is *the* most sensitive spot you can kiss.

Tips for ear kisses

- Kiss the ear as if it were a mouth. *Smack, smack, smmmmmmack!*
- Kiss the earlobe as if it were a lower lip: suck it and nibble on it, occasionally tugging on it with your lips and teeth.
- Gently insert your tongue into the ear. Trace the ridges and hollows with a light touch.
- Make little *mmmmmmmmmmmmmm* and *uhhhhhhhh* sounds. Heartfelt *oohs* and *aahs* are also a turn-on at this time.
- Breathe softly into your partner's ear. The sound of your breathing will be exciting. The tickle of your lips and of your warm breath will be a unique delight.
- But be extremely careful about the *volume* of the noises you make when speaking or breathing directly into some-

one's ear. The lowest whispers you utter are capable of being magnified into booming sounds that can startle or even hurt your lover.

• Whisper things to your partner. Appropriate comments include such phrases as, "I love you," "You're so sweet," and "Oh, darling." A really nice thing to say at this moment is, "I love your ears."

Advice for men

A word to the wise. For many women, a kiss on the ear is about ten times more arousing than a kiss on the mouth.

Do you like to be kissed on the ears? If so, how do you like to be kissed?

WOMEN:

"The ears are one of my favorite spots. If someone hasn't tried kissing someone's ears, they are missing out BIG time. Again, I think gentle is the key. Don't breathe directly into someone's ear because it's LOUD! and use your tongue lightly—don't just stick it in there—all you get is a wet willy. And don't forget about the area around the ear, the hairline, behind the ear (!!!) and the back of the neck . . . they're all connected."

"NO!!!!!!!!!!!!! Stay away from my ears!!!!!!!!!!!!"

"Yes, gently and dry. And not outdoors."

"Yes, as long as it's not too wet."

"I like it very much! I especially like to have my earlobe nibbled on, and a tongue in the ear can be very sexy."

"Yes, but without tongue."

"Love it! Gentle but firm lips, a little bit of sucking and pulling, maybe the tongue slips inside, not too much saliva but damp is okay. I love to have my lobes sucked on."

MEN:
"Yes. So does my partner. Light nibbles interspersed with lavish lip work . . . mmm. Sprinkle this with a few open-mouthed, hot-breath whispers, and va-voom. We're off!"

"Yes! Fantastic! Lick me behind my ears, under my earlobes, stick a tongue in my ear, and I'll follow you home."

"Slight sucking of the earlobes does it more for me."

"Yes! I like my earlobes lightly nibbled, and long tongue strokes on the outer edges."

"I love having my ear lobes nibbled on, and especially like her to lick inside and put her tongue in my ear canal."

Kissing Tip

By watching and listening to how your partner reacts, you can learn a lot about exactly which parts of their ears they like kissed best.

The
$\mathcal{N}$ECK KISS

"I was fifteen when I had my first intense kissing encounter. I was sitting in the den with my boyfriend, and I was getting very excited while he was kissing my neck. It was the first time I had had my neck kissed in this way. I was moaning quite loudly and getting very turned on, and my boyfriend asked, 'Are you all right?' I felt I had to explain why I was so excited."

The most surprising thing that the kissing survey revealed was that (aside from the mouth) of all the places that women like to be kissed, their favorite spot was the *neck*. More than 97 percent of women rated it as a highly erotic zone. And while nine out of ten men also liked to be kissed on the neck, none of them came close to raving about it the way women did. Conclusion? Kiss her neck! And, gals, if he doesn't know by now, tell him. Imagine some poor fellow going through his entire marriage not knowing that his wife is driven wild by neck kisses?

Do you like being kissed on the neck? If so, what do you like most about it?

WOMEN:
"OOOOOOOOOO Yeeeeeeeeaaaaaaaaaaahhhhhhhh!!!!!!!! It gives me warm fuzzies all over . . . it really turns me on."

"You get chills or goose-bumps all over your body."

"To have a man come up behind me, breathe on my neck, bite me, and kiss me there is to send a thousand volts through my spine."

"Oh Lord, I hate it. Just kidding! Along with my ears it's my favorite. I'm not quite sure what I like so much about it. It just feels amazing."

"Kissing, licking, or biting my neck is an incredible turn-on."

"I go crazy when someone kisses my neck. *That* is very sexually arousing to me."

"Drives me nuts!"

"Yes! My neck is super sensitive. I like the tickly passionate feel of someone's teeth nuzzling my neck, their little sucking movements, everything! I don't like guys who bite hard or hoover my neck. Good neck kisses don't leave hickeys."

Kissing Tip

To avoid hickey marks on the neck, massage the neck with your tongue instead of biting or sucking it.

MEN:

"Heck, yeah. Call it a throwback to caveman days, but there's something strangely intimate and trusting in letting someone lavish oral attention on your neck (noting that in the animal kingdom, that's the part you gotta protect from all attacks). It's soft, sensitive . . ."

"Yes! It's like acknowledging that there is more to the body than just the face and lips."

"It's something pleasant, a sensation of being captured."

"There's a certain power that the kisser has in this position which makes me feel excited—a certain something about not being able to return the kiss (except perhaps in the person's hair) and having to store up one's erotic responses."

Do you ever kiss your partner on the neck? What technique do you use?

WOMEN:

"Yes, yes, YES!!! For lack of a better term, my current lover and I (he's not my boyfriend, kind of one of those in-between types) are both neck fanatics (vampires, perhaps?). Kissing, using your tongue as you would on someone's ear, even nibbling and biting are good. Watch the biting though, some people don't like it and some bruise easier than others. An often overlooked place is the Adam's apple and right below, down to the collarbone and where the neck meets the shoulders. And do *not* forget the back of the neck—oh my!"

"A little biting can do wonders."

"Yes, firm kisses, a little bit of biting, trailing my tongue along their jugular or Adam's apple and along the jawline."

MEN:

"Little wet kisses up the throat to near the ears while holding the back of her head gently. On the back of the neck, I like to stimulate the hairs around the hairline and on the spine. Electrifying!"

"I kiss her and slide my lips all over her neck, kissing along the way."

"Since I don't like to give hickeys (or receive them for that matter) I like to gnaw at a woman's neck by folding my lips over my teeth and sometimes using a little tongue action in between."

"If she's lying down on her back, I'll kiss and lick from her Adam's apple up to the underside of her chin, or else from the shoulder to ear (sideways sitting position) or after sweeping her hair away, the nape of her neck up and around to behind her ear."

How to kiss the neck

1. After a few lip kisses, drop down and kiss the side of the neck. This move ensures a smooth transition from lip to neck kisses.
2. Place tender kisses in the hollow of the neck, which is that small cuplike depression that the chin touches when you bend your head all the way forward. Then lick that little cup as if you were drinking from it.
3. Exhale your warm breath onto the back of your lover's neck as if to mark it for a kiss. Then bite and kiss the spot.
4. Strange as it may sound, you can study pictures of Dracula to get more pointers on technique. For example, in the film *Taste the Blood of Dracula,* Dracula (Christopher Lee) faces the woman and with both hands

on her shoulders leans down and bites the side of her neck. In another scene he stands behind her, his right hand on her right shoulder, his left hand pinching the left side of her neck, while he prepares to bite the right side of her neck. The same positions can be used for tender kisses or playful love nips.

The

ℰLECTRIC KISS

Whenever I lecture at colleges or universities, I'm asked more questions about the electric kiss than probably any other single kiss. "Is it really possible to give my boyfriend an electric shock when I kiss him?" they want to know. Not only do I tell them that the answer is yes, but also we shut off the lights and get two volunteers to demonstrate it right in front of the audience. Here's how you can do it, too.

How to get charged up with static electricity

First shut off the lights. You'll see why in a moment. Now rub your feet back and forth on the rug. It's not necessary for your lover to do the same; one charged party will suffice for this kiss. When you rub your feet on a rug, you build up an excess of negative electric particles and become negatively charged, primed for a small electrical shock when you touch something or someone who is positively charged or uncharged—that is, electrically neutral.

Now slowly approach your boyfriend. You must be careful not to touch him with any part of your body, because if you do you'll neutralize the electrical field and the sparks won't fly when you kiss.

At this point your lips are getting closer to his and in the dark you can barely see his face. You have to be careful. Listen for the sound of his breathing and use that like an airplane pilot uses a homing signal to guide the plane into the airport. Home in on his breathing. At this crucial and romantic moment, you may want to whisper a few amorous words to him, such as:

"Hold steady now. Don't move."

This will ensure that he is in position for your kiss. Move in slowly, ever so slowly. Part of the fun of this kiss is getting close and intimate without touching. Can you do it? It takes a bit of will power and even a bit of practice.

As your lips close within a fraction of an inch, a tiny electric spark will jump across from your lips to his. If you're looking down at this precise moment, you'll see a scintillating flash of light, like fireworks. This is the electricity that poets and novelists have written about for years. And now for the first time you and yours have made it all visible. Sparks of love! The excitement of the moment is usually enough to cause some young lovers to jump back in surprise. But you are a hardy soul and forge ahead. If you have been listening intently, you will have even heard the tiny crack and pop of the electricity as it jumps from your puckered lips to his. Now is the time to lean forward and kiss him. For right now your lips are tingling with a spent electrical charge, and there is no better relief from the tiny electric shock than the sweet sensation of a soft kiss. Ah!

Where to do electric kisses

One young woman told us that she tried the electric kiss on her boyfriend after a party when they were standing in the hallway to go home. The air was dry and there was a big shag rug on the floor. The conditions were perfect. The shock was so strong that the fellow jumped back and wanted to know whether she was hooked to an electrical gag. He was afraid to approach her until she explained what she was doing. Then he couldn't get enough of it. They stayed there for twenty minutes shocking each other with what seemed like lightning bolts from their lips. She reported that his mouth felt so tender and sweet after the shocks that she was tingling for hours afterward. This illustration suggests that the setting for the electric kiss must be just right. If you pick the setting carefully, your experience will not only be shocking but also highly romantic.

The electric kiss will work in the following locations, each of which has been rated by a master electrician in volts. (Ratings from 55 to 1,000 volts will give you a nice, harmless shock, not enough to hurt you by any means. Ratings over 1,000 volts can be slightly painful.)

On a couch	55 volts
In a movie theater	66 volts
On a shaggy rug	625 volts
In a hotel lobby	800 volts
In a department store	75 to 1,000 volts
Under a wool blanket	250 to 4,000 volts

The
$\mathcal{B}$ITING KISS

"I had to buy a whole bunch of new turtleneck shirts," said a twenty-year-old woman. "One of my boyfriends bites me and gives me so many hickey marks when kissing that I have to cover myself or my other boyfriend will notice." Ah, the pleasures—and dangers—of the biting kiss!

Almost all lovers like to bite and be bitten while kissing. So don't shy away from using your teeth. The Internet kissing survey revealed that 78 percent of men and 84 percent of women like to be bitten (gently!) by their lover when things get passionate. Said one man, "A little nipping kiss turns me on and tells me she's turned on, too."

The biting kiss is at once sophisticated and sensual, playful and serious. It's a kiss of affection, of deep desire, of controlled aggression. Every lover should master it fully; whether or not you like to do it, you should know how it's done, just in case the urge comes upon you to bite—or be bitten.

How to deliver a biting kiss

1. Gently nip your lover's flesh between your front teeth.
2. Tug up a fraction of an inch.
3. Release the flesh and let it slip back through your teeth.
4. As you release the flesh, move immediately in toward the skin again and nip the flesh between your teeth once more.

Kissing Tip

You can vary the kiss by nipping the flesh between your lips only, so that your teeth don't directly touch your lover's flesh.

Do's and don'ts of the biting kiss

Do:
- Be gentle.
- Nip deep enough into the flesh so that you can actually tug at it with your teeth. If you're careful it won't hurt. Prolonged execution of this kiss can scratch, however, making the skin sore. Use your judgment as to when enough is enough.
- Do be aware of your inner reactions. The biting kiss can arouse subtle aggressive feelings within you. Psychologists and poets have told us that love involves some element of aggression, and the biting kiss will let you get in contact with it in the most playful way. At the same time, recipients of the kiss can get in contact with their feelings of submissiveness and subservience. These feelings are part of the normal give-and-take of any love relationship and can be experienced during the biting kiss in a safe context.

DON'T:
- Don't try it on a first date. Know your lover before you venture into the realm of the biting kiss.
- Don't draw blood, or don't draw an excessive amount.
- Don't try the biting kiss through clothes, only on bare flesh. If you try it through clothes you'll just get your mouth full of lint.

Do you like to bite or be bitten when kissing?

WOMEN:
"A little nip may be tolerable, but that's all."

"I like to be bitten gently on my neck."

"Yes, especially on my neck and ears. Wow!"

"Yes, yes, yes, both. I admit I do like to bite a little. Not so much on the mouth but certainly on the neck."

"I like biting and being bitten when kissing, but it's got to be gentle."

MEN:
"My partner bites all over, including my tongue and lips. But I'm not too excited about it."

"I love my lower lip to be bitten when being kissed. I could playfully bite my partner for hours."

"Yes, if kissing other parts of the body besides the lips."

"A nibble or a tug here and there is nice. I like having my earlobes tugged at, or little half-bites around the collar."

If you're reluctant to try the biting kiss, consider only one thing. Have you ever seen two puppies rolling around on the floor biting and nipping playfully at each other? When you bite your lover you regress to a primitive level and sex becomes freer and more liberating. Engaging in a little aggressive loveplay, teasing each other now and then with biting kisses, can get rid of a lot of inhibitions. Just remember to stock up on turtleneck shirts.

The
$\mathcal{C}$ANDY KISS

"We almost got thrown out of a restaurant once for spitting all over the table when we tried it," said a nineteen-year-old woman from Texas. "We started laughing uncontrollably at the wrong moment. See, we started passing sweet green peas from my mouth to his. Then he tried to squirt some of his iced tea into my mouth. That's when we had the accident."

Control and practice is the key when doing this classic kiss. And it is truly a classic. In fact, according to anthropologists, when our ancestors transferred food from mother's mouth to baby's, the custom of kissing itself originated. So when you really get to know your partner and are willing to regress to an infantile level, it's time to try the candy kiss.

The term "candy kiss" describes any kiss that contains something sweet in it, usually some candy that the lover passes directly to the mouth of his or her partner. It's a kiss for sensual lovers, requiring a sensitive palate and a willingness to overcome that initial disgust at the idea of sharing candy, food, or drink from your partner's mouth.

The *right* way to do the candy kiss

1. When you're eating candy, discuss its taste with your lover until your lover becomes very curious about it. Then show your lover what it looks like by opening your mouth. Don't overdo this, and do it only with hard candies—unless you know the other person *very, very* well.

2. Be observant. When you're sitting in a restaurant let your eyes dart furtively at your lover's smile, at the lips, at the teeth. All these quick visual images are food for love. They will excite you, make your passion grow; they will ignite a keen and ardent desire within your heart. You will feel yourself powerfully compelled toward your lover. You will have hardly any appetite for food because you'll be so preoccupied with your lover's looks. When your partner laughs, let your eyes flick quickly to the interior of the mouth. Look at the tongue. Note the sparkling nectar that covers it. Such views will ignite a powerful thirst within you that can be quenched only by kissing—tasting—your lover's mouth.

3. Finally, pass candies from mouth to mouth. Some lovers like to pass chocolates, others prefer hard candy. There are hundreds of different candies you can use.

Do you ever eat food or candy from your lover's mouth?

MEN:

"Once in Paris this girl came up to me and kissed me and she had a mouth full of champagne and she spit it into my mouth and that was really nice. It was the first time anything like that had ever happened to me. That was one of my most memorable kissing experiences."

"Any food (or other material) passing from mouth to mouth is generally nicer if it isn't too wet, so highly slobbered candy is a definite no-no in my book. Fruit (especially stone fruit such as peaches, apricots, etc.) tends to transfer rather nicely, as do cherries, dark chocolate, and various other goodies."

"We've held food between our lips or teeth to feed the other, to get that touching of lips that must occur when sharing food in this way."

WOMEN:

"I love to kiss while drinking wine. Tasting the wine on my lover's tongue is wonderful!"

"We've sipped wine and passed candies. Not food, though; that's a bit disgusting."

"We pass gum back and forth."

"I like to exchange hard candy during a kiss."

"Almost every night after dinner I put a chocolate mint on my lips and make my lover grab for it. We always get a laugh out of this."

"My lover likes to chew ice cubes, and he's fond of sharing them with me."

The
SLIDING KISS

One survey response came from a fellow in his late twenties who said that when he was four years old his baby-sitter used to kiss him. She was a good friend of the family, almost like an aunt to him, and she baby-sat during the summer, usually wearing a sleeveless dress and watching television with him beside her. One day she asked him to kiss her, and he started kissing her face and mouth, which she liked. "But she wanted me to kiss her so much," he recalls, "that I had to think of some way to do *new* kisses because constant mouth and cheek kisses used to bore me, so I started to *slide* my mouth down her arms. She was rather chubby, and I enjoyed kissing the flesh of her arms. Then I'd slide my mouth all the way down to her hands and I'd kiss her hands. She thought it was a great game. I called it the sliding kiss."

He may have invented this one when he was four, but he's admittedly still at it. "I do the kiss with my girlfriend now, and she likes it, too."

So go ahead and *sliiiiiiiiiiiiiide* all across her body. Be as risqué as you want. Slide down the neck and shoulders, and kiss along the way. *Sliiiiiiiiiiiide* down her legs, too, stopping to put itty-bitty kisses on her teeny-weeny toes and then slipping and sliding all along her back. *Mmmmmmmmmmmm, smmmoooooooooch!*

Subtle sliding kisses

Once you perfect the longer slides (for example, down an entire arm), you're ready for the small, subtle variations. During a routine lip kiss, slowly slide your mouth from side to side. *What is this guy up to?* Take it nice and slow and savor your lover's mouth first from one angle, then from another.

The psychology of the sliding kiss

Some species, including horses and humans, regress to an earlier stage of development when making love, which is why lovers often call each other "baby." Knowing this fact can help you become a better sliding kisser. Don't think of kissing as a serious adult activity; instead think of it as a childish game. Study one-year-olds and you'll learn a lot about how oral a human can be. Were we *really* that way at one time in our development? More than that, on some deep level we're *still* that way; and when you get your lover to express this childish side, you'll succeed in unleashing his or her fullest erotic potential. So go ahead and *sliiiiiiiiiiiide!*

Places to slide-kiss

People like to be kissed in the darnedest places. Here are some suggestions from the survey. Slide to these spots and kiss:

- "I like to be kissed in the crook of the arm."
- "My shoulders!"
- "Between the fingers is nice. Toes too!"
- "I like being kissed directly in my armpit."

The
WET KISS

One day I received a call from a young man who said he wanted to ask me some questions about saliva.

"My girlfriend says my mouth is too wet when we kiss. I love kissing her, but she says my kisses are too sloppy. Can you give me some advice?"

"Why don't you try swallowing your own saliva when you kiss? Call me back in a few weeks and tell me how it's working out."

A few weeks later he actually called back.

"I did what you said about swallowing my saliva and that worked okay and she stopped complaining about my kisses being too wet. But the truth is that I like *her* saliva so much that I want *her* kisses to be wet. I was too embarrassed to mention this last time we talked. Am I . . . you know . . . perverted?"

"Listen, you're not perverted. You're just one of those people who loves wet kisses. But don't worry. There are lots of people who love wet kisses more than you could ever imagine."

In fact over 90 percent of respondents to the Internet kissing survey said they liked wet kisses at least *some* of the time.

Do you like both wet and dry kisses?
"I like dry initial kisses, but wet kisses later. Affectionate kisses shouldn't be too wet. Sexual kisses are wet."

"I don't like slobbery wet kisses ever. But moist dewy kisses are great. So are dry soft lips."

"Dry is better. A little moist is great, but soggy and wet is gross."

"Depends on the circumstance and the mood. Wet kisses are generally more passionate and reserved for the bedroom or other fairly intimate or intense moments."

The
ᵁ N D E R W A T E R K I S S

"Kissing a woman underwater has been one of my most ardent fantasies since puberty," writes a young man from New Jersey. "However, most women I've spoken with on the subject didn't seem eager to try this most romantic osculatory twist. In fact only one agreed to try it. We were in a hot tub alone and feeling quite romantic. After I suggested we experience some liquid-enhanced passion, we submerged and enjoyed a brief French kiss. Unfortunately some of the chemically treated water in the tub leaked into my mouth and my girlfriend was totally unimpressed. While we embraced and kissed on the water's surface during future swimming dates, making out underwater was definitely dry-docked."

A surprisingly large number of men and women (about 50 percent) said they liked kissing underwater, although very few of them seemed to have perfected the technique. The following instructions were given to me by the young man from New Jersey.

How to kiss underwater

1. First of all, you and your partner should orient your-selves in collar-bone-high water by facing each other.
2. Hold each other and hold your breath.
3. Commence kissing and slowly submerge a few inches below the surface.
4. Do not interrupt your lip lock.
5. While kissing, remember to enjoy not only your part-ner's lips and tongue, but also the sensation of the wa-tery cocoon all around you.
6. Rise for air as needed, then resubmerge.
7. When under water, kiss gently to conserve air.

Kissing Tip

Kissing in the shower also qualifies as an under-water kiss and is *very* popular with both men and women.

Do you like to kiss underwater or in the ocean or pool or in the shower or bathtub?

WOMEN:
"Not underwater (yet . . . you've given me some ideas), but in a pool, yes. Chlorine is a little off-putting. Shower or bathtub, yes, but not for long as it's too arousing and leads to other things very quickly."

"Yes . . . underwater—it makes me laugh, so it's more of a game."

"Kissing in the shower, with the water rushing down, mingles all the saliva and sweat together and makes things a lot smoother."

"Certainly in the shower. It can be very sweet with all that wet. Men seem to find this more thrilling, though, than I have."

"I like to shower with my lover and wash his hair and then lean against the cold wall in the shower and kiss one of those long, slow kisses."

MEN:
"Whenever I was on a date at the beach we did it. It's shorter because it's only while you hold your breath."

"Taking a shower together and kissing sends shivers up my spine."

"In the shower we love to hold one another, kissing and caressing the other's body."

"I developed a technique that I call the Mermaid Interception Surprise Technique (MIST). This works well if you are too embarrassed to discuss underwater love with your partner. Encourage her to swim under the water. I personally find the sight of a woman swimming underwater to be supremely arousing, particularly if she has loose hair floating and swaying in the currents. Swim after her and make sure that your body is parallel to hers (usually horizontal) and you are facing each other. Reach out, embrace her and kiss, all while both of you are in a horizontal plane."

The
Smacking kiss

Late one night I awoke suddenly to strange sounds. *Squeak! Boing! Squeak! Eek! Eek! Boing-boing-boing! Squee-ee-ee-ee-ee-ee-ee-eek!* I peered from my bed in the dark at the air duct vent, which sometimes played strange jokes on us, wafting sounds from room to room. I was getting a very clear transmission from the couple who lived upstairs. *Boinnnnnnnng! Boinnng! Boing! Squeak! Squeak! Squeak!*

What the hell is going—I sat up in the darkness. Then I heard a woman's voice. "Oh," she was saying. "Oh-oh-oh-oh-oh." It didn't make any sense to me, and I began to curse the architects.

"Shut up!" I yelled. "Be quiet up there!" All to no avail.

Squee-ee-ee-ee-ee-ee-ee-ee-ee-eek! Boing! Boing! Boing! The sounds continued. And the woman was stuttering "OH!" faster than ever.

Suddenly it dawned on me, and I felt sheepish about having yelled at them.

But my neighbors didn't pay attention to me anyway. They certainly didn't care who heard them, and neither should you. Whether it's the sounds of a bed squeaking or the lip-smacking sounds of kissing, the music of passion can be fun to make and hear. So, if you've ever been embarrassed or self-conscious about the little noises kisses make, forget it! Three out of four people surveyed actually enjoyed the natural sounds of lip-to-lip service and considered those smacking noises erotic and stimulating. One person in five also liked making little inarticulate *oohs* and *aahs* and hearing their partner make them too when in the middle of kissing. Some people like a natural kissing sound; others prefer a more exaggerated noise. Vary your style until you and your partner find the sounds you like best.

Do you like the noise kisses make?

WOMEN:

"I love the sounds of the mouth, teeth, tongue, and saliva, and also the noises emitted from us from being excited. They increase the intensity I bring into the kissing."

"I like the sounds of kissing, together with silence or nature in the background: the wind, birds, distant traffic, children playing, etc."

"If we're alone, the answer is a big YES—it's a turn-on."

"Yes, if they're incidental and not intentionally exaggerated."

"Yes, I love it. The noise is a great turn-on."

"I like the noise if it's *me* making it—I don't like listening to other couples."

The
$\mathcal{L}$ IP-O-SUCTION KISS

Lisa, a thirty-three-year-old woman from Illinois, was going out with a guy from Michigan for several years before she experienced this one. She was sitting on the living room couch when her boyfriend, Bob, began to kiss her upper lip passionately. As he sucked her upper lip in a teasing and flirting manner, she simultaneously began to suck his lower lip.

"We were fooling around and feeling playful and got hooked," she says.

The name *lip-o-suction* originated as a pun on *liposuction,* the medical procedure of removing fat from a person's body by sucking it out through a tube. But the lip-o-suction kiss has nothing to do with the medical procedure. The only similarity between liposuction and the lip-o-suction kiss is that sucking is involved in both—in the lip-o-suction kiss the man sucks the woman's upper lip while she sucks his lower lip.

"What a trite name!" commented a young man from Hawaii. "Kinda takes the romance right out of it. But I always enjoy this kiss."

The lip-o-suction kiss is actually thousands of years old.

The *Kama Sutra* says it is accomplished when a man kisses the upper lip of a woman while she in return kisses his lower lip. The modern version adds a *sucking* action to the kiss, a highly sensual element that gets the two lovers intimately involved with each other's mouths.

One twenty-five-year-old woman from Arizona said, "It's a brand new kiss in America, popular because it's something new and requires the use of the lips instead of just the tongue." A thirty-five-year-old woman from Florida said she thinks the kiss is becoming more popular "because people have seen it in movies and on TV recently." As I mentioned earlier, I learned about lip-o-suction from a teenager's description and drawing, and many high-school and college students have told me they regularly enjoy this kiss.

How to do the lip-o-suction kiss

1. The man begins by gently sucking the woman's upper lip.
2. While he's doing this, his lower lip is between her lips, so she can gently suck his lower lip.
3. Both parties continue this sucking action for many minutes without interruption. The longer the kiss, the more erotic it becomes.

Why does the *man* suck the woman's *upper* lip? Perhaps there is a physiological reason: Some Vedic texts suggest that there is a connection between a woman's upper lip and various lower erogenous zones. If this is true, it may also be that there is a similar connection regarding a man's lower lip. At any rate, it is certainly possible for the couple to vary the kiss by simply reversing their positions.

What special instructions can you give to those who want to try the lip-o-suction kiss for the first time?

"When doing this for the first time, you should be gentle and not aggressive. Try to gently caress your partner's lip with your two lips."

"Try to make sure you keep the suction going between you and your partner for at least five seconds at a time."

"It's fun unless your partner starts to play Can You Top This!"

"It's a fun way to get to know one another. And you'll learn if he's interested in you or not. The way your partner does his or her lip-o-suction tells you a lot about the person."

Kissing Tip

Try sucking in the lip to a set rhythm, such as every two or three seconds for a hypnotic, sensual effect. As a twenty-year-old student described it, "I like sucking her lower lip in short pulses in between my lips, and it's really a turn-on when she sucks back at the same time on my upper lip."

Standing in a doorway after a wonderful evening together, you decide to kiss your boyfriend good night. You begin innocently enough with a regular kiss, but suddenly your mouth slips down until you're locked onto his lower lip while he sucks your upper lip. You draw him in actively, pulling his lower lip deep into your mouth. It tastes like an apricot—only it's softer! Meanwhile you can feel him passionately swallowing your upper lip. So that's the way he wants to kiss! Well, two can play at this game. Now it's a little tug-of-war between you, a brief wrestling with the lips. You never knew he was so insistent! He never realized you were so wild and uninhibited! Your heart is racing, your lips are throbbing, and you can't tell where your face ends and his begins.

Before long you each feel that strange erotic presence that seems to hover over lovers in the midst of lovemaking like the fluttering of the wings of birds. A thousand impulsive thoughts rush through your mind. How long will the kiss last? What if you lose control? Will your lips stretch permanently out of shape? What does it mean now that you've kissed this way—so close, so sensually? What's he thinking? Will he consider you a loose and immoral woman? But he's sucking your upper lip like a madman himself!

Then, mercifully, a blissful feeling rises from your toes and melts through your blood so that you're not thinking, you're simply kissing more passionately than ever. And you don't even care if you lose control. Your eyes close as the lip-o-suction continues. You relax into the kiss, now letting him take the lead, now reasserting control yourself.

Lip-o-suction. It may sound funny. It may even feel funny. It will certainly do funny things to you.

The
$\mathcal{T}$EASING KISS

After a while kissing can get too serious, and even the most staid and stuffy lover will tell you there comes a time when you need to do something out of the ordinary to reduce the monotony that creeps into a repeated activity. The teasing kiss is a kisser's kiss, the one to turn to when all other kisses have been kissed, when your lips feel like cardboard and your tongue is tired and dry, when you're about to throw your hands up in despair and scream: "Kissing isn't all it's cracked up to be!" The teasing kiss introduces something out of the ordinary into overly serious necking.

How to do the teasing kiss

1. Begin by kissing a few times so that you establish a rhythm of kisses to the point where your partner expects another one.
2. Break lip contact and wait for your partner to lean toward you for the next kiss.
3. Timing is important here. As your partner leans forward, you must lean forward also, *but don't allow your*

lips to touch. The purpose of leaning forward is to draw your partner onward, to mislead him or her into thinking that another kiss is imminent.

4. Just before your mouths meet, lean back quickly, and just far enough so that your partner can't reach you with a kiss. Move with speed so that your lover is tricked.

5. If your partner smiles and gets feisty, you know you've done it right.

Some people misinterpreted the whole idea of the teasing kiss. Said one woman, "No. I don't like to be teased; therefore, I don't do it to others. That's mean." Certainly a real tease can be mean, but playful teasing is a part of lovemaking. And some men, trapped in a role they think is masculine, can't let themselves be playful. One young man from Spain said, "No, I don't tease because it's too typically feminine."

Kissing Tip

A variation of the tease is the pause, where you wait a second or two before returning your partner's kiss. Watch their eyebrows go up in frustration as you withhold the expected return kiss.

Do you ever tease your partner with a kiss?

WOMEN:
"Guilty as charged."

"Sometimes I wait before returning a kiss. It's fun to play cat and mouse."

"Yes. He can be teased by my kissing his mouth and pulling away before he fully responds."

"I've teased and this can be very erotic. Once a man held me back from kissing him; he would kiss me and then wait quite a while before kissing me again. He prolonged our pleasure that way, hovering over me and sensing my excitement."

MEN:

"I get close enough, and then pull back before the kiss is given, to make my partner want to give it even more."

"DEFINITELY! That's fun!

"The most simple form of torture is where you *don't* do something that she wants, but you're really close and you could kiss her, but tease her mercilessly."

"I use the tease technique because it's exquisitely excruciating. The longer you hold out, the more enthusiastic the eventual 'catch!' "

The
ℬUTTERFLY KISS

"And we're there on the couch, side-by-side, and she's got her face up next to mine and I'm feeling really peaceful and drowsy, when out of nowhere comes this fluttering sensation like a butterfly's wings brushing up against my cheek, this infernal ticklish sensation that sends a sort of vibration through me. If I didn't know better I would have thought a soft puppy was in her place or a feather or the petals of a flower trembling on the breeze. So I look down at her and do you know what she was doing? She was sort of laying there with her cheek touching mine and she was simply batting her eyelashes at me like she was flirting with me, only her eyelashes were so close they were touching my cheek and brushing up and down and making me feel so funny all over I just wanted to hold her in my arms and squeeze her and never let her go. 'What are you doing?' I said. She looked up at me and said, 'It's a butterfly kiss, Clayton, and it means I love you.' I'll never forget it."

Without doubt, the butterfly kiss can make any intimate kissing session memorable. It's easy to do, too.

How to do a butterfly kiss

1. Put your face close to your partner's cheek.
2. Flutter your eyelashes against your partner's cheek by slowly opening and closing your eyes.
3. Vary the kiss by fluttering your eyelashes slowly against your partner's neck or eyelashes.
4. Remember to do it slowly and make sure your eyelashes are touching your lover's face. If it's quiet, you can actually hear the sound of the eyelashes brushing against the skin.

Do you ever give your lover a butterfly kiss? What advice can you offer for those trying it for the first time?

WOMEN:
"Usually it's in conjunction with sleeping with them, sort of a sexual afterglow activity because it requires the person to be relaxed and still for a while. It's very delicate. Be relaxed and wait for a quiet time to try it."

"I like brushing my eyelashes against his neck. It helps if you laugh while doing it."

"I think people have liked it because I have long eyelashes. Still, it seems men need more direct touching than that, so a butterfly kiss may be a good wake-up technique. Get really close and blink as fast as you can."

MEN:
"I usually do this when I'm in a playful mood. Don't get too close to the face. Stay far enough away so that the eyelashes just touch."

"This is a nice snugly kiss for me, when I'm in a romantic mood rather than an all-out sexual mood. It's a friendly way of showing affection and being close to my partner without being too vigorous. My only advice is to make sure the recipient stays relatively still so as not to poke any body parts (e.g., ears, nose, etc.) into the eye of the kisser."

"It's fun and always brings a giggle."

"Although I've never used my eyelashes, I do lightly brush my fingertips much like a butterfly kiss. I guess my advice on *that* would be to make as light a contact as possible for maximum effect."

"It feels bizarre if you push your right/left cheeks together, getting literally eye-to-eye, and blink at each other. I discovered this kiss on my own. As far as advice? Hmm. Well, *necks* are rather receptive, too. And *belly buttons,* but this might go beyond your definition of *kiss.*"

Kissing Tip

Keep in mind that 75 percent of men and 40 percent of women have never experienced a butterfly kiss. So you can often give your lover a pleasant *surprise* with this one.

The
$\mathcal{L}$ONG KISS

The longest kiss listed in *The Guinness Book of World Records* lasted an amazing 417 hours. Although you needn't set a world record, keep in mind that longer kisses are generally more erotic than shorter ones. Your lover will be delighted when he finds that what he expected to be a short kiss turns out to be a long, deep one instead. And if you can kiss for four or five minutes straight, you're doing better than 95 percent of your friends and neighbors. Survey results reveal that most people kiss for only a minute before breaking lip contact.

How to perfect the long kiss in five easy steps

1. Kiss your lover squarely on the lips. You must begin with the basics, and a good solid kiss is the foundation of the long kiss.
2. Prolong the kiss until you feel somewhat breathless. Part of the fun of this kiss comes from the slight feeling of breathlessness that occurs at the outset.
3. Now breathe in through your nose. This step is the

trickiest. If you find it impossible to breathe through your nose, you'll have to break off the kiss and start again at step one.

4. Listen for the sound of your lover's breathing. This is another joy of the kiss. Since the two of you are breathing through your noses during the kiss, you'll be able to hear each other's breath and you'll get some sense of each other's emotional state.

5. When necessary, swallow, but don't break lip contact. In this way you can prolong the kiss for many minutes without interruption.

Do's and don'ts of the long kiss

Do:

- Be passive at times and merely keep your lips in contact with your lover's lips. In other words, simply stand together with your lips touching. Although this may *sound* dull, I guarantee that it will make your day! You will feel the keenest electric shocks coursing through your nerves and all up and down your body.
- Get used to kissing for long periods of time. This kiss offers a unique opportunity for uninterrupted and constant mouth-to-mouth contact with your lover.
- Combine this kiss with the French kiss and other types of kisses. One of the benefits of learning the long kiss is that it can be combined with virtually every other kiss. And by combining the technique with other kisses you can prolong your favorite types of kisses indefinitely.

Don't:

- Don't panic. Some people get anxious during long kisses because they feel they're suffocating. Just remember to

breathe through your nose and your panic will subside.
- Don't hyperventilate. Some people get so excited that they begin to breathe rapidly. This excess breathing introduces too much oxygen into the bloodstream and can make you dizzy. Relax and enjoy the kiss and breathe normally through the nose.
- Don't gasp for air when you break lip contact.

How long do your longest kisses last?

MEN:
"When it's quite dark and cool, when we're close and drowning in love, well . . . a few minutes at least. Warm breath—by nose or otherwise—is an aspect of long kisses I could definitely get used to."

"About forty-five to sixty seconds. Usually seven to ten seconds."

"I guess it could go for a minute, one nice long kiss."

"A couple of minutes."

"Three minutes."

WOMEN:
"Until I run out of breath."

"My longest kiss lasted about one-half to three-quarters of an hour. That was with my first boyfriend. I like kisses over one minute long."

"Maybe a minute?—as long as I can breathe and there's some variation. Actually I'd probably prefer running a lot of kisses together."

"My longest kisses last four to five minutes. I love long kisses! The length of a kiss depends on the type of kiss and our moods. The kisses range from pecks (one second) to

French kisses (four to five minutes). I tend to do more French kissing, and these are longer-lasting for me than closed-mouth kisses. I'd say the average length of a kiss is twenty-five seconds."

"Usually two or three minutes per kiss. I like them to last as long as possible."

Long kissing sessions

In addition to long kisses, many people love long kissing sessions. Also known as necking sessions or simply making out, the length of such activities can vary widely. Some people get bored rather easily with kissing, perhaps because they don't know many different types of kisses. By becoming familiar with the different kisses in this book, however, you'll be able to lengthen your necking sessions so that they last entire afternoons, entire evenings, entire dates. Ah, what bliss! What unending, excruciating joy!

Advice for men

Survey results reveal that, in general, women like longer kissing sessions than you do. As one man put it, "I don't like long kissing sessions too much; if it doesn't lead to something else, I get bored." But if you kiss her for longer periods of time than you're used to, you'll be on the right track and you'll find she gets more aroused.

WOMEN:
"In my opinion, you're wasting your time if you don't kiss for at least twenty minutes."

"Sometimes kissing (just kissing) lasts for an hour or two and continues through making love. Other times my lover and I will kiss all night and save making love for the morning."

"Ten to fifteen minutes is an easy stretch—fully clothed. But naked it is less. I like long kisses in places where you cannot *do* anything else."

"I usually engage in kissing for only about from two to five minutes with my husband before we have sex."

"I don't know how long, but I know I love to 'make out' for hours."

"I have had marathon kissing sessions—like four hours—not one continuous kiss, but a very intense session. I enjoy this as long as it doesn't get routine."

"Some kisses have started all-night kissing sessions. One friend and I started kissing at 9:00 P.M., and we kissed all night until 3:00 A.M."

"One time I kissed a friend for approximately seven hours—no foreplay, just fun kisses. It was excellent!"

The
$\mathcal{P}$UBLIC KISS

They pass by and look and sometimes they even stop and stare and then they move on again. And all the while you hardly notice them because you've wandered off in your mind to a place where the palm fronds are always swaying in the breeze and the kisses are always sweet. These people who pass by while you kiss in public don't bother you at all; they're like shadows on a hot summer day when you haven't got a care in the world. The crowd seems to melt into the background, and all that's left is this delicious sensation as you and your lover kiss on a busy sidewalk, at a shopping mall, or on the beach.

The public kiss is very popular in the United States, where about 95 percent of respondents said they've enjoyed doing it. Our worldwide Internet survey indicates there is considerably more public kissing in Europe, especially in Italy, Spain, France, and Portugal. A twenty-three-year-old woman who had visited a dozen European countries said people kiss everywhere. "I studied in Germany for six months and my friends and I used to laugh about how intimate people would get in public. I don't consider myself to be conservative, but some of what I saw, I would rather not have seen, if you know what I mean!" According to another young woman, "We should approach kissing the way the Europeans or French do. French girls many times do oral kisses in public on the *rue* or square or park. Nothing is ever thought about it."

Kissing in public requires only a modest bit of courage. Usually no one interferes, although passersby may glance over to see what you're doing.

There are lots of good reasons for kissing in public. Here are just a few:

- You simply can't wait to get somewhere private.
- You're saying goodbye at a train station or airport.
- You enjoy being affectionate and you don't care who sees.
- You're at a party and other people are necking, so you get turned on to the idea and do it too.
- You're an exhibitionist at heart and like to have an audience for your kissing.

How to kiss in public

1. Make sure you're standing in a place where people won't bump into you. The two best places to stand on a sidewalk are up close to a building or right at the curb.
2. Take a quick glance at the surrounding crowd to make sure no one's about to walk into you.
3. Step close to your partner.
4. If your partner doesn't look immediately receptive to a kiss, say something to let him or her know what you're going to do. In a crowded bowling alley one December, a young woman told a boy, who was wearing green pants and a red hooded jacket, that she wanted to kiss him because he had on Christmas colors. Then she kissed him in front of everyone.
5. Kiss your partner boldly and without shame.

Things to avoid in giving a public kiss

- Don't do it to excess so that other people feel uncomfortable.
- Don't get paranoid.
- Don't make an announcement to the crowd.
- Don't excuse yourself. Why should you? Virtually everyone kisses in public at some time or other.
- Don't grin and gawk at passersby after the kiss. If people look at you, simply ignore them. They may be picking up important pointers for use in their own public kisses.

Do you ever kiss in public?

WOMEN:

"I'm not timid about showing affection in public, and it's fun to get caught. Sometimes I feel a bit like a show-off, sometimes special, sometimes embarrassed. I watch for my husband's reaction."

"Yes, I do kiss in public. One time my boyfriend came to pick me up from work. He rushed over to me and proceeded to kiss me. I gave him a peck. He wanted a longer kiss and I let him know I didn't want to. My boss was in the room. It was a very informal work setting, yet I was still uncomfortable. I generally like pecks in public, although I do have fantasies about kissing him passionately in public. Passionate kissing is very private for me. I'll kiss passionately in a car or if I'm sure no one else is looking."

"Before I emigrated to the United States from France, I'd kiss in public at parties, and I felt great."

"I prefer discreet, quick kisses."

"A particular man finally grabbed me in a restaurant (while we were enjoying a glass of wine and the tension between us) and kissed me very passionately. I was embarrassed *and* extremely excited. What was exciting was that his passion overrode any sense of his surroundings."

"In public places, but not in public. I feel excited to steal a kiss in a public place—clandestine kisses are very exciting."

"I've grown up disliking other people's PDAs (public displays of affection), so I don't do it myself. On occasion I'll give a short kiss."

"I was brought up never to show *any* affection in public. But I have kissed in public anyway."

"I wouldn't want to make an exhibition in a public place. But if you were meeting your lover after a lapse of time, for example, at an airport, it would be completely natural to kiss intimately and openly. I always enjoy being kissed in public."

"I come from England where we kiss instead of shaking hands."

"We never clinch kiss in public, but we give each other pecks all the time."

MEN:
"Indulging on the dance floor (while dancing, that is) during a slow dance is . . . yum."

"I have kissed in public. Usually the girl is a little bit more embarrassed, but I guess it could be the other way around. I never paid any attention to the people in the area, never noticed whether they stopped and stared. I don't generally mind if I see other people kissing in public. When I was in France I saw a lot more of it."

"Love to. Feel proud and somewhat sneaky. It's a way to proclaim to everyone that you dig each other."

Kissing Tip

Most people (94 percent) like being kissed in public, as long as the kiss isn't too intimate or deep.

The wedding kiss

Your first kiss as husband and wife may be the most important public kiss you'll ever do. Hundreds of people, scores of photographers, and the eyes of history may be upon you at that moment. No need to worry or lose your nerve. Take a quick look at the crowd, then kiss with these pointers in mind:

- Make it a kiss for you and the guests who are watching. The kiss should last a long time; you want to give the photographers a chance to check the exposure and click away. Meanwhile you're kissing away.
- Men, don't be afraid to lean her back, Hollywood style.
- Women, lean back like Scarlett O'Hara for a full photo.
- Choose the spot for the first kiss beforehand.
- No French kissing—it doesn't show up on film and there isn't enough time to get warmed up for a French kiss.

"It wasn't memorable," said one nineteen-year-old newlywed. "He kissed me as we were leaving the church, and there was nothing particularly romantic about it."

Many people said that their first kiss as husband and wife took place in a most uninteresting setting. To remedy this, arrange for a romantic place that you'll remember for years to come. Try to have a professional photographer on hand to capture the moment. And make it a long, deep, soulful kiss that expresses all your feelings.

One woman who had her wedding kiss recorded on film said, "That photo summarized everything we felt for each other and has become almost a yardstick to measure all our subsequent kisses."

The
ℳ USIC KISS

Molly is twenty-two years old, and she wears a walk-woman (that's what she calls it) when she kisses, because she kisses . . . to music. She's outside the library this after-noon waiting for her boyfriend Richard, and she's listening through earphones to loud rock. When she spots his crew cut over the crowd of students, her heart begins to pound like a tom-tom, and she turns the volume down but not off to hear him say hello. Then they're alone behind the library surrounded by all the green of summer, and the music fills her ears again.

In the inky glass doors she sees the reflection of her yellow radio clipped to her shorts. With one hand she changes the channel, recognizing snippets of lyrics, passing classical and pop stations, until she locks in on a love song that was very popular a few years ago, one with a strong beat, so that when she puts both hands around Richard's waist she's kissing to that love song. She watches the red reflection of his shirt blend into the blond reflection of her legs in the glass as she kisses him. Richard is such a sweet guy, and he kisses so divinely, his lips tender and soft and exploring. And as the music becomes more insistent, he rocks her back and forth in his arms, kissing her with long breathless kisses that send shocks one after another over her body and through her blood until she's numb with a fainting feeling all through her nerves and through the extremities of her limbs. And then the music starts pounding in her ears, a new song about true love that she likes, and it takes her up and away, and she rises on her toes to snuggle into Richard's kiss, going further and further into him as if drawn inward by the beating rhythm, lovely Richard with his crew cut and his sweet kisses that never seem to end—oh, how they blend into the music and make you go inside yourself and then outside yourself to that never-never land. She falls into the kiss like a rock sinking deeper and deeper into a bottomless pool until she's blind and unconscious and transformed somehow so that she knows that even when the song ends and she blinks open her eyes, she's not going to be the same, she might not even be Molly anymore. Some part of her will always be lost in that kiss, lost in a fathomless pool from the bottom of which Richard is calling to her—Richard and the music together calling from the unseen depths.

The music kiss can unleash emotions, make you feel romantic and sexy, and evoke moods you thought you'd never feel again. It requires being aware of how music can affect your mood, and then letting the mood evoked by the music influence the sensation of the kiss. Whether it's blues or rock on a walkman, jazz or classical on a stereo, or country music on a car radio, 95 percent of lovers reported that they occasionally liked to listen to music while kissing or having sex. Only 5 percent said it interfered with their kissing concentration.

The primary variant of the music kiss—the rock kiss—is probably the most physically demanding kiss ever. The following instructions may introduce you to a new dimension in multimedia heart-jolting excitement known as slamming-jamming rock kissing or simply rock kissing.

Rock 'n roll! Music madness. Drive yourself right over the wall! If you don't like it, it's probably my fault for not explaining it right, but I did the best I could—this *is* a tricky one.

How to do rock kisses

♫ Put on loud rock with a driving dance beat.

♫ Have your partner lie on the floor. Lie on top of your partner and look at him or her. Feel the rhythm. You can also do this standing up.

♫ Rock is usually a four-four beat. Kiss your partner on the fourth beat, wait three beats and kiss on the fourth again. Continue kissing only on the fourth beat.

♫ After a while, kiss on the second *and* fourth beat.

♫ Finally kiss on *each* beat. This is fast and furious kissing—but when the music gets into your blood, there's nothing like it.

♫ For added madness, tilt your head to the left for the first kiss, to the right for the second, and so on.

♫ Add your own kissing syncopation by pausing for a few beats and then kissing your partner only on the fourth beat or only on the eighth beat. Surprise them! Your kissing will become as unpredictable as music itself.

MEN:
"I like to kiss with background classical music. It's very pleasurable (if neither Bartok nor Ives)."

"Listening to music on a walkman while kissing is like going to a Pink Floyd concert."

"I like kissing while listening to slow love songs on a walkman."

WOMEN:

"Yes, it can be a lot of fun and very sensual if it's the right kind of music, with crescendos."

"Sometimes you can kiss harder when there's a loud drumbeat."

"I like to kiss to Gloria Estefan in my kitchen!"

"When kissing I especially like slow and sensual music, or fast and throbbing, or sweet and melodic, or sentimental. Or any kind."

"I listen to music when kissing in the car."

"Kissing with music is great because you have more desire, more emotions, you feel excited because you have the music inside; you feel inspired."

"I kissed once with a walkman on and it was distracting. When my boyfriend had the same song on as me it was nice; but then we changed channels and I was listening to a love song and he was listening to heavy metal and it was weird."

The
ᘁ PSIDE-DOWN KISS

Good kissers are always fantasizing about kissing in creative ways. In their imagination they toy with *all* the possibilities. And eventually they may begin to wonder, "What if I kissed my honey bear *upside-down?*"

Luellen is that kind of creative soul. Twenty years old, infatuated with her second cousin Hank, she's been flirting with him for two weeks. This evening she's with him by the pool. No one else is around. It's a strange and forbidden kind of pleasure she feels as Hank lies back on a plastic chaise lounge and she sits beside him. He's so nonchalant and cool it's maddening!

She adjusts her one-piece bathing suit. Now her hip is so close she can feel the warmth of his thigh. Ever so slowly she leans over him and their bodies finally touch. His brown eyes hold hers in a torpid stare that seems to draw her down toward him. Closer and closer she bends until finally their lips are touching and she can actually taste the chlorine on his mouth. She's kissing him at last!

But then her blood begins to run fast with the thought that she shouldn't be doing this. After all, he's her second cousin, and even though she knows they'll never take it any further than a few harmless kisses, their families might object!

She breaks off abruptly.

"Stay put, Hank, I'm going to kiss you upside-down!"

He blinks up at her.

"Hunh? What are you talking about?"

"Just don't move. Keep your head where it is."

She gets up and goes to the back of the chaise lounge and stands there for a minute, looking down at him. His brown hair is tousled, his dark eyes holding hers. But from this position—with his head totally upside-down in relation to her—he doesn't look like Hank anymore! So she takes courage and bends down over him again. His mouth is so inviting from this angle! And he's looking up at her like a startled puppy. He could be anybody, now. He sure doesn't look like her cousin anymore! How free she feels now that his face is inverted! How excited she is as she kneels down at the head of the chair and kisses him upside-down!

Her head is spinning and her pulse races. His mouth feels so different! The upside-down kiss is perfect, absolutely perfect for moments like this when you're engaging in a semi-forbidden kind of kiss! The entire experience seems dreamlike and fantastic. His kisses are so new, so different! And it's the newness, really, that makes her heart pound. The newness and the feeling that at any moment they might be discovered! In fact, she feels she might be discovered by *him* if she were to go back and give him regular right-side-up kisses! He might think twice about kissing her. If he saw her face the normal way, he might remember that they're distantly related and he might want to stop. These upside-down kisses are saving her!

After a few minutes she's so excited she has to stop and catch her breath and *think* about what she's doing. In fact she may have to reevaluate her *entire life* now. Keep in mind that once you've tried a few upside-down kisses, no normal kiss will ever feel the same. And any kissing partner will seem *extra special*. She steps back and looks down at Hank's upside-down face. His dark moist eyes are like spilled ink, gazing dreamily up at her with a stunned expression that she can't decipher—because it's like no face she's ever seen before. It's upside-down!

The greatest pleasure of the upside-down kiss is this element of the new and the strange. Familiar faces suddenly become unrecognizable. It's the perfect kiss for lovers who've been married for years and who want to add some zest into their kissing. And if it adds zest for these lovers, imagine what it can do if you're just starting out in your relationship?

How to do upside-down kisses

1. Ask your partner to lie down.
2. Kneel at their head and lean over until your forehead is over their chin. Their mouth will be right in front of your eyes.
3. Move up so that your eyes are directly above your partner's chin and your mouths are touching. Your upper lip will touch his or her lower lip when you kiss.
4. Try a French kiss in this position. You won't believe how different it feels!
5. Break off now and then and gaze into your lover's eyes—right from that upside-down position! You won't be able to read each other's expression very well!

A young woman wrote to say she discovered this kiss when playing spin the bottle. Her boyfriend was standing over her and she was on the floor. He leaned over her and was face-to-face with her, upside-down. "He put his lips to mine and we were kissing. Then it turned into a French kiss. It was fun trying to kiss like that and finding tongues and all."

Some lovers who tried it found it awkward or uncomfortable. Because upside-down kisses are done from an inverted position, it's important to maintain your own sense of balance. The trick here is to select a good position for leaning over your partner. Kneeling on a bed can be a restful position. Try also lying on the floor and propping your chest up with pillows.

Kissing Tip

A futon or rug is an excellent surface on which to try an upside-down kiss because it's low to the ground.

Do's and don'ts for upside-down kisses

- Don't become confused just because your lover is upside-down.
- Don't worry about the fact that you have somewhat less eye contact with your partner in this position. Lack of eye contact will be more than made up for by increased tongue contact.
- Do tell your lover how good he or she looks upside-down.
- Do switch positions, so that sometimes you are lying down and your partner is leaning over you.

Did you ever kiss upside-down? If so, how did you like it?

MEN:

"It's not easy to accomplish anywhere but lying down, but definitely worth it. Particularly when tongue is involved . . . very strange sensation."

"I don't generally enjoy this kiss. It is too much like looking up the other person's nose."

"I've tried it. It's fun, playful, and silly."

WOMEN:

"This is a weird one. Unless you're just kissing someone's forehead briefly, it's very disconcerting. Usually one of us would turn around PDQ."

"I love upside-down kisses! They're the most outrageously fun types of kisses I've ever done. Definitely different and worth a try now and then!"

Once you've mastered the upside-down kiss, you'll want to work a few of them into your kissing sessions whenever possible. Before you know it, you'll be looking at people and wondering, just wondering, what they'd look like if they were standing on their heads. Wondering, just wondering, what those mouths would feel like if *you* were kissing *them* upside-down!

The
SURPRISE KISS

Remember how Hannibal used the tactic of surprise to defeat the Romans? He crossed the Alps in the winter of 218 B.C. on elephants! The defenders were so surprised they suffered a stunning defeat at the hands of the great strategist. So too will your sweetheart, not expecting your surprise kiss, fall like the Romans at Cannae, and in the battle of love victory will be yours. Inscribe within your heart the motto, "I am the Hannibal of lovers," and you'll surmount any obstacles to romance, for nearly 100 percent of men and women love surprise kisses.

How to give a surprise kiss

1. Wait for the right time. Just as Hannibal attacked when no one believed he could, so should you deliver your kiss when she doesn't expect it: early one morning, when other people are present, or maybe when you're shopping together.
2. Surprise your lover in a place where you usually don't kiss.
3. Use tactical distractions to enhance the surprise. Tell her she has nice earrings and then, while pretending to examine them, plant kisses on her neck and shoulder.

Do you ever like to surprise (or be surprised by) your lover with a kiss?

WOMEN:

"I like to surprise and be surprised with a kiss. It's an unexpected yet welcomed show of affection. I feel special."

"Yes, I love both. I'll come up behind my boyfriend and kiss him on the neck and cheek. I've also done this and had this done to me during the middle of a conversation."

"Although I hate surprises in general, to be kissed for no apparent reason other than because you want to at that moment is nice—but it should be quick."

"When the relationship is new, it's hard to know when the next kiss is coming. An old boyfriend kissed me quickly when he was introducing me to his friends for the first time. That made me feel so wonderful inside."

"Yes, sometimes I think he's not thinking of me, and then he'll come in and kiss me."

"One day I was in a clothing store alone. My lover walked up behind me and surprised me with a kiss on the back of my neck. It's still memorable after ten years."

"It's nice to be kissed unexpectedly when I'm lying in the sun on the beach. Or when I'm half-asleep and my husband wants to get me awake to make love."

"In the gym my lover walked across a crowded room of women and kissed me passionately while I was trying to do leg presses. He returned coolly to his weights. I continued exercising, but my heart was thumping like a machine gun."

"I love when he comes up behind me when I'm working in the kitchen and starts kissing me on the back of my neck."

"Yes—anytime, anywhere—magic. . . ."

"I absolutely *love* to come up to people I love from behind and give them a bear hug and kiss on the neck or cheek! I also love to wake up (or be woken up by) my lover with a kiss."

MEN:
"Yes, when you least expect it because it's crowded or not the typical time or place for a kiss."

"Yes, to say 'I love you' while dancing."

"Yes, just to catch her by surprise and see how she responds."

"Yes, first thing in the morning to wake my mate up—starting slow on the toes, or elsewhere, and ending on the lips."

"Yes, on the nape of the neck, usually. But softly on the lips as well."

"When you can't resist the temptation!"

The
$\mathscr{V}$ACUUM KISS

Imagine that you're sitting with your boyfriend on the couch, but neither of you are watching television. You're wearing a new silk blouse, and he's told you three times this evening that you look stunning. Finally he leans forward to kiss you. After a few minutes you're necking seriously, and you begin a long kiss, during which your lips adhere tightly to his. Slowly and playfully and without even thinking about what you're doing, you begin to suck the air out of his mouth. What a feeling! His lips taste like the inside of a peach, and as you draw his breath deep into your lungs you can feel your souls mingling. Then he begins to suck the air out of your mouth, and by the time you've given him every atom of breath you have, you feel like you're so totally and completely his that your nerves are vibrating with shameless excitation. You've let him take your very life's breath away! How together you are at last! How mystically close! And on some level how profane and wicked it feels! Like Hylas in the pond with the nymphs, once you've acquired a taste for vacuum kisses, they'll take you deeper and deeper beneath the surface until you're lost in all their myriad charm.

Types of vacuum kisses

In a double vacuum kiss you keep your lips sealed tightly together as you both suck the air out of each other's mouths simultaneously. Your cheeks may actually hurt from the intense pressure exerted on them.

In the reverse vacuum kiss, you just touch your lips together—no tongue or teeth involved—and blow back and forth into each other's mouth.

In the mouth-to-mouth vacuum kiss you hold your partner's nose and then blow air into his lungs as if you were resuscitating him.

Kissing Tip

About 60 percent of respondents never experienced this kiss, so it's a good one to spring unexpectedly on your lover. If it doesn't work at first, tell your partner to breathe *out* while you breathe *in*, and that should get things started.

Do you ever suck air out of your partner's mouth?

WOMEN:
"I hold his nose and blow air into his mouth so that it fills his lungs."

"Only someone I really know well."

"I've been married one year, and I do this once in a great while. Sucking air out of your lover's mouth seems to be something done by new lovers, who tend to experiment more."

"Yes, he hates this."

"Yes! I also return the air. Sometimes it's only our lips touching—no tongue or teeth involved, and we're blowing back and forth into each other's mouth."

"It's not fun at all when done with a lot of force. But when done gently it can be enjoyable."

"It feels weird, but I like it. It takes quite a bit of practice."

MEN:
"It's very exciting to have this done to you."

"And how! If we're feeling really adventurous, we play *chicken suck*—who can hold the pressure the longest! (We haven't turned blue ever, okay?)"

"It's such a turn-on. It's like she's giving herself totally to me when we suck air back and forth, and I can't think. I just love it."

"The vacuum kiss is a must! You simply suck the air out of your partner's mouth and watch them make a funny face."

"I hate when someone sucks the air out of my mouth. You can also blow air into someone's mouth. It kind of hurts but it's funny."

"It's different but sexually arousing. The partner who receives the kiss gets a blast of air in the beginning until the person runs out of air. Then it's a warm mist."

The
$\mathcal{P}$ERFUME KISS

Chances are you've encountered this one on your own without even knowing it; perhaps like this . . .

In the afternoon sunlight you check your curls in the mirror as you wait for your nails to dry. You're wearing blue cotton pants, a topaz-yellow blouse, white sneakers, and matching yellow socks. You notice the time and run into your big sister's room and ask her frantically if she has any perfume you can borrow. She points to a little amber-colored bottle with a label written in a foreign language. She's talking as you splash it on hurriedly without even time to smell it or listen to her, and then you move.

You're out the door and halfway to the street, where Tommy's car is parked, before the scent catches up with you. Hold on! It rises to your nose in slow, insistent waves and you suddenly know you used too much. But you can't do anything about it now. *What did she say? It's a French perfume and it's stronger . . .* Then you're sitting beside him; he's driving to your favorite picnic spot, and even though the windows are down you're constantly aware of this woodsy floral scent. What *was* that stuff? When he parks, the fragrance fills the whole car, and you're mortified even as you notice that this smell has layers to it, luscious woodsy notes on top, and beneath them a heavy musky fragrance that lingers like the refrain of a sad song. Tommy kisses you, and as he does the odor seems to change, giving the impression that the air contains something like talcum powder. He inhales deeply, saying you smell delectable, delicious, sexy, naughty. And indeed you do. Suddenly you give yourself over to his kiss, and the fragrance which at first seemed merely musky now becomes pungent; almost imperceptibly the odor begins to resemble the emanations that rise from day-old underclothes. He's kissing you with a steamy passion, and your senses are numbed as layer after layer of the intoxicating fragrance fills your nostrils and penetrates deep into your lungs. Your sister never prepared you for this! He kisses more insistently than ever, his lips wandering deep into the hollow of your neck, seeking the source of that deliciously intimate aroma.

So goes the perfume kiss, *a kiss in which any sensual odor plays a part*. But this is merely the start. It's a kiss with as many subtle variations as there are fragrances. Still, of the thousands of fragrances you can perceive, perhaps none is as exciting as the smell of your lover's hair or arms or neck. Indeed, throughout history the most passionate lovers have been those most sensitive to human smells. The Emperor Napoleon loved the unwashed smell of his wife so much that he would write to her from the battlefield and tell her not to bathe for a week so that when he got home he could enjoy her natural body odor. When the poet Goethe traveled, he took along his lover's bodice to be reminded of her scent. And when one of H. G. Wells's mistresses was asked what she liked about the overweight, unattractive writer, she said he smelled of honey.

Many survey respondents said that the smell of their lover was often the greatest natural aphrodisiac, more powerful than any perfume. It's no surprise that perfumers often try to duplicate human smells and regularly use animal scents like skunk, civet, and musk to give a sexual tinge to their creations. Even some vegetable scents are sexually stimulating; the smell of yeast, baked bread, beer, fresh tobacco, cut grass—all act as mild aphrodisiacs, reproducing as they do some natural human scents.

Unfortunately, the majority of smells are anathema to modern society. It's even difficult to talk about the subject since our language has no words for most of the smells you can perceive. When you're told every day by advertisers that you must deodorize yourself and eradicate all body odors, you begin to get the message that natural smells are bad. So you'll probably have to coax yourself and your lover into trying the perfume kiss.

How to do the perfume kiss

1. If your lover is wearing perfume, breathe it in deeply before, during, and after each kiss.
2. Embrace your lover and inhale the natural fragrance of the hair, the sweat, the flesh itself.
3. Kiss all up and down your lover's body, stopping at any interesting smells along the way. Be fearless about encountering strong smells, but if you come across a smell you don't like, simply move on to the next.
4. When you reach a smell you *do* like, tell your lover! And keep on kissing.

Kissing Tip

Press your nose to your girlfriend's neck just under her ear—this is a spot where most women apply perfume—and sniff repeatedly and quickly like a dog on the scent until she cries with tears of laughter, then kiss her rapidly all over her neck and face.

Do you enjoy kissing a person who is wearing perfume?

MEN:

"Some perfumes are too overpowering, but some are *very* nice."

"Yes, it adds another dimension. If the perfume is strong it repels me. If it's just enough to detect, and only here and there, it adds to a person's natural scent, which I usually enjoy."

"I love the way she smells! When I kiss her sometimes I'm like a hound dog, sniffing and kissing all over her body, and getting turned on as I come across different odors, whether natural or artificial. I especially love smelling under her arms. Sometimes when she's going away for a while she'll let me borrow one of her undershirts so I can be reminded of her by its odor. And I hate when she uses a deodorant. It kills all her sexy smell.

"Her perfume sort of puts me in a daze. Soft and light is just great."

"I love the smell of bare skin, even sweat . . . mm."

WOMEN:

"I enjoy my husband's natural body odor."

"Perfume can increase my *intensity* and the type of kiss I deliver. It's exciting to move around the body and stop at a smell. This also applies to natural body odor. I have a very sensitive nose."

"I love kissing someone who's wearing fragrance."

"The smell of cologne can help stimulate arousal, but it normally *tastes* lousy."

"A faded cologne on a man can be very pleasurable. It must be faded, though. It has to be blended into his own scent, which hopefully is great."

"For me, kissing is a five-senses type of thing, and kissing a man who is wearing a good cologne is so exciting."

"I don't really like deodorants, talc, aftershave. The smell of a clean man is more than enough to drive me wild."

"Even when he isn't around and I smell that cologne, I always smile."

"I have an extremely good sense of smell, so I always recognize events, people, etc., by their smell. I like cologne if it's had a chance to blend in with the person's natural scent, if it's not too strong, and if it's constant (i.e., you smell that cologne and instantly think of the person). This will sound silly, but fabric softener—Downy, Bounce, whatever—is the *best* cologne there is."

"I like recognizing the smell of a person."

"The natural smells of a person's hair, body, and mouth remind me of people a lot more than perfumes or other cues do. I remember a few months ago giving an old friend a long kiss and the comfort and memories it brought back were all wrapped up in the clean line-dried scent of his clothes and the familiar old lemony shampoo smell of his hair."

The
$\mathcal{R}$OLE-PLAYING KISS

Imagine that you're Cleopatra kissing Caesar in the great palace at Alexandria. Exotic incense wafts through the royal bedchambers, morning sunlight streams down from the high windows, and silk sheets await you and the ruler of the Roman Empire. What kisses you could kiss if you were king and queen of the Nile!

Or imagine you're a widow living in the Old West, and you're standing outside the bank on a hot afternoon. Suddenly a man on a black horse rides up in a swirl of dust. A moment later you're on the horse beside him. Now the two of you are galloping out of town. Your friends and neighbors stand staring in the street. The scent of leather and gunpowder fills your nostrils. The horse slows down and finally you're alone with your secret lover—the outlaw from Dodge City. You get off the horse and he takes you by the hand and leads you under a tree. You look up into his eyes in the shadow of his black hat. With a sardonic sneer on his lips he takes you into his arms. No words are needed. You know what you're there for. No one can see the two of you now. But even if the world were looking, you couldn't stop yourself. Your heart is beating fast. The sun feels warm on the back of your neck. Yesterday is gone. Tomorrow doesn't matter. All that matters is what's in your heart, and that tells you to do only one thing.

Kiss him!

Kiss him and forget everything else. Kiss him as if you would die for him. Kiss him as if your blood and his were running together through your lips.

But kiss him!

Everyone has yearned to be someone else, if only in dreams or daydreams. In role-playing, these fantasies somehow free your creative and emotional side, bringing fire and passion into kisses that would otherwise feel ordinary and dull. A role-playing kiss is any kiss in which one or both parties make believe they're someone else by introducing an element of pretense into the situation.

There's no limit to the different kisses and scenes you can develop. Don't worry about losing your mind or becoming someone else permanently. When the kisses stop and the dust clears, when the gold tables and silver jewelry vanish, when the FBI stops following your car, you'll be yourself again, same as usual—with only one difference: you'll have kissed a kiss the likes of which no one has experienced for hundreds, maybe thousands of years. Here are just a few of the role-playing kisses you can try:

Slave and master

WOMEN:
"We pretend to be slave and master sometimes."

"This is something I haven't done, but I may try it with a suitable partner."

"I've done this, but not recently. It's a lot of fun, but tends to push buttons!"

"There were occasions when I *felt* like a slave to someone. This giving-in can be luscious. But maybe, sadly, it's not pretend enough."

"In my head sometimes I pretend I'm a slave to him."

MEN:
"No, I don't like that—but she likes to have me be forceful and be a real man."

"Sometimes we adopt exaggerated dominant and submissive roles, telling the other, 'Talk dirty to me,' or demanding that the other reply, 'Yes, sir!' or 'Yes, ma'am!'"

Prostitute and customer

WOMEN:
"I pretend to be a prostitute or stripper every now and then. The kisses that follow are usually a little more aggressive or deeper."

"I haven't done this yet—maybe in the future."

"I pretend I'm a prostitute sometimes in my fantasies."

The androgynous kiss

Almost 98 percent of the people I surveyed found the idea of switching sex roles mentally while kissing—the androgynous kiss—difficult to even consider. But a young woman wrote to tell me she tried it with her boyfriend. "His reaction to the kiss when I pretended I was a man was basically, *Wowie!* It was very revealing to our relationship, provoking lots of conversation that continues."

If you're brave enough to try it, you may gain some

insights into how your partner perceives the whole kissing experience. The kiss is rather easy to do. You just mentally try to imagine what it's like to be a member of the opposite sex while kissing. You don't even have to tell your partner what's going through your mind.

Do you ever pretend to switch sex roles while kissing?

MEN:

"Sometimes I'm active (dominant) and sometimes passive (submissive) in my sexual moves toward my lover, and this varies, depending on the time and mood I'm in."

"Pretend? No. But there are plenty of role reversals! I enjoy being pursued, having the other take the lead, as much as I enjoy pursuing. I feel a relationship has to be give-and-take. So sometimes she's in charge and doing the work and giving me pleasure, and other times I do the work, give direction, etc."

WOMEN:

"Yes—but this really requires trust—and is very challenging. Sometimes it's just in my head."

"I've wondered what it would be like to be a man kissing *me*. I've wondered this because I'd like to know if I'm a good kisser."

"I've tried to imagine I'm a man kissing a woman. Is that sick or what! . . . I've got the supposed upper hand— taking control of the kiss, handling the hair, jaw, etc. It's good."

The gangster kiss

It is early morning, and you and your lover are standing on the sidewalk outside the bank. The streets are almost deserted. You have one hand in your jacket pocket on your .38 automatic. At the curb Vito is sitting in a black Ford with the motor running; he's smoking a cigarette to calm his nerves. Your partner is looking up at the tall glass buildings that mirror the blue sky. You turn to her and notice a strange romantic gleam in her eyes. Perhaps it's only the reflection of the bank. She takes a breath to bolster her courage, and her white teeth flash. Without thinking you bend down and kiss her roughly on the lips. Suddenly her mouth feels like the softest and most beautiful thing in the world. Your heart is beating fast, your head is swirling, and you almost forget that in a few minutes you'll either be rich or dead. . . . You have just succumbed to the gangster kiss.

Because gangsters live outside the law, they're not hampered by rules and restrictions; they live the way they want to and enjoy a greater degree of freedom than most people. Their methods of kissing can teach you how to have fun and feel free. And since they often risk their lives, gangsters are usually filled with a high-strung anticipation and nervousness that can overflow into their sex lives and make their kissing urgent and erotic. They know they may be dead tomorrow, and as a result they routinely kiss with a fervor that would sear the lips of the lawful.

Do you ever make believe that you are criminals?

WOMEN:

"Once at a costume party I dressed up as Al Capone, and it was fun. When I kissed my boyfriend I laughed right in his face."

"The more aggressive you pretend to be the more passionate the kissing becomes."

"I pretend to be Madonna because she has a rebellious attitude. Sometimes I dress and act outrageously like she does."

"I sometimes make believe I'm the gangster's woman and I wear a really trashy dress. My boyfriend acts rough, and it's an escape from the civilized world for me. No domesticated man can compete with him when he's that way."

The gangster kiss is by far the most creative type of kiss. It demands both a killer's ruthlessness and a lover's sensitivity. It is one of the most formidable weapons in Cupid's arsenal, and once you master its subtle intermixture of fact and fantasy, your love life will never be the same. Every meeting with your lover will be as memorable as a blackmail threat, every date as exciting as a conspiracy, every kiss as stimulating as a bank robbery.

The
$\mathcal{F}$RIENDLY KISS

"I'd really like to kiss more of my friends," Sandra was saying to her husband.

"Male friends?"

"Yes. Why are you looking at me like that, Chuckie? I'm talking about a purely *friendly* kiss."

"On the cheek or mouth?"

"Well, *ideally* on the mouth."

"You're crazy!"

"Why?"

"Because guys will get the wrong idea. You're young and beautiful and they'll never be able to kiss you platonically."

"Still, I'd *like* to. I feel I'm missing out on something."

Sandra's dilemma was brought to my attention after the first edition of this book appeared. She wrote and explained that there was one very important kiss I had neglected to include—the friendly or platonic kiss. Here's how she described it:

"I think you should discuss another type of kiss between men and women; a kiss with little or no romantic meaning attached to it. I love to kiss my male friends when I can. I'm sorry more of them don't understand that a kiss can be a purely friendly gesture. Because men don't realize that a kiss can be *just* a kiss, they expect more when you kiss them. But that ultimately backfires and works against them, because I'm afraid to kiss them in a purely friendly way."

It's true that kisses between men and women in our culture are almost always associated with romance. As a result of this preconceived idea, most people forego the pleasures of kissing friends of the opposite sex who are physically and emotionally attractive to them. But when done properly, the friendly kiss gets around that dilemma.

Kissing Tip

This kiss could get out of hand unless you're careful to make sure it *remains* platonic.

How to keep a kiss purely platonic

If you're married or have a lover, begin with step one. If you're *not* currently in a relationship, begin with step five.

1. The first step is to admit openly to your *lover* that you have a *platonic friend* of the opposite sex. Answer any questions your lover may have about your platonic relationship. Assure your lover that you have *no sexual interest* in your friend. Offer to introduce your lover to your friend if they haven't already met. If you *do* have any sexual interest in your platonic friend, admit it openly, but swear repeatedly that you can restrain yourself from acting on your sexual feelings. You must believe what you are saying and you must convince

your *lover* of this fact before you can move on to step two.

2. Once you've established that you have a platonic friend, tentatively suggest that you'd like to express your friendly feelings with a *chaste little kiss*. This may be difficult to explain, but it's well worth the effort. Stress the fact that you have no intentions other than giving your friend a platonic (nonsexual) kiss. By talking it over with your *lover* beforehand, you'll actually defuse some of the danger inherent in any kiss between male and female friends. If you handle this discussion correctly, you'll also build trust between you and your lover at a time when trust is most needed.

3. Be prepared for the inevitable jealousy that will arise when you announce that you'd like to kiss someone else.

4. Ask for your lover's *permission* to kiss your platonic friend. You could also offer to do the kiss in your lover's presence (say at a party) to prove that it will not lead to any other sexual acts.

5. Most people don't discuss whether a kiss is going to remain platonic. They simply kiss and hope for the best. It may help, however, to discuss (with your platonic friend) the fact that you want the kiss to remain purely friendly.

6. Kiss your platonic friend in public, so that there is less danger of the kiss leading to anything else.

7. If possible, arrange to have your lover present when you kiss your friend.

8. Keep your first platonic kiss short and sweet.

> ### Kissing Tip
>
> Avoid French-kissing platonic friends. As one twenty-five-year-old male put it, "My one rule is—no tongue except with SO's (significant others)!"

Would you like the opportunity to kiss more members of the opposite sex without having to move on to other sex acts with them?

WOMEN:
"I do now. I know when someone is making more of a kiss than I am, and I can usually disentangle myself from that situation right away. I'd like it if more men here in Canada thought kissing was a singular activity though."

"No. I like to lead into sex with kissing. If you are going to kiss me, you'd better follow up with more later on. Don't start something you can't or won't finish!"

"It can be fun. Yes."

"For those who can be platonic about their kissing, that's great. Kiss more people. Start a revolution. Life is grand. I think if more people kissed platonically, the world would be much happier. Same goes for hugging."

MEN:
"I kiss anyone it doesn't bother. I'm a mad hugger, too. My friends are close . . . there's no sexuality implied. Heck, I kiss my same-sex friends, and so do my women friends."

"Sure I would, but, to be honest, I think after a period of time, if it was a girl I liked a lot, it would have to move on to other things."

"I truly believe kisses can remain platonic. And I also believe that the more kissing of members of the opposite sex, the better."

How popular are platonic kisses?

Our new survey indicates that 91 percent of women and 80 percent of men are convinced that a kiss *can* remain purely platonic. Still, most people (64 percent) *never* attempt this kind of kiss. Of the 36 percent who do, most (95 percent) don't discuss whether the kiss is platonic or not beforehand. Men and women overwhelmingly agreed about one thing—*two out of three respondents wish they had more opportunities to enjoy platonic kisses with friends of the opposite sex without having to feel pressured to move on to further sexual contacts.*

Do you ever kiss friends of the opposite sex (a "friendly kiss")? Can such a kiss remain platonic? Do you discuss the fact that the kiss is strictly a friendly kiss? Is a kiss just a kiss?

WOMEN:
"Yes kisses can remain platonic. It usually helps if both parties define how they see such activities. I tend to discuss it with people I kiss. Not all kisses are just kisses though. A lot of the time platonic kisses are a sort of testing ground in which you decide if you really are attracted to someone or if the relationship should remain on a friendship level. If someone makes a big deal out of asking me if they can kiss me, I *know* it isn't just a friendly kiss—there are ulterior motives behind the request."

"No. Hell no! So I don't even try it. I know I will want more. NO, NO, NO, NO. And still I say—NO!"

"Sure. I was involved in a very touchy feely organization in high school, so all my friends and I still kiss each other hello and goodbye and such with no problems—and we don't have to discuss it. I think it's usually pretty obvious when a kiss is platonic or not."

"No, I don't kiss platonically, but if men kiss me on the cheek it is usually okay."

"I suppose a kiss can remain platonic, but then what's the point? Besides, I think it's usually such an intimate act, unless it's directed to a family member, that I wouldn't feel comfortable kissing a friend. In my opinion, a kiss *isn't* just a kiss."

MEN:
"Yes, I kiss friends of the opposite sex platonically, and I believe such kisses *can* remain platonic. We don't discuss per se the fact that it's platonic because there's little suspicion between us. If it will make someone uncomfortable, I don't . . . but if not, I do it when I can."

"Some kisses are just friendly—no pressure, no tying emotion . . . some are so much more."

"When I kiss women platonically it is never on the lips."

"On the lips? You don't know women. I never kiss women who are just friends on the lips or they'd become more than friends. I don't think a kiss can remain platonic. No kiss on the lips is strictly a friendly kiss; at least in our western culture. And a kiss isn't just a kiss. To kiss a girl is like saying you love her."

"I sometimes give a friendly kiss. And yes, they can remain platonic. We don't discuss it. It's just assumed that it is platonic."

> **Kissing Tip**
>
> If you find your kisses with your platonic friend getting out of hand, the best advice from couples counselors is to sit down with your *lover* and explain the situation. You may find that the two of you can pick up where you and your platonic friend left off.

PART THREE

Kisses from Around the World

The
$\mathcal{F}$RENCH KISS

This is the most intimate, sensual, and exciting kiss, and yet up until now there have been no explicit descriptions of it for lovers to study. Young people interested in the French kiss, also known as the soul kiss or tongue kiss, have had to rely upon chance or luck in perfecting it. Typically lovers stumble upon the kiss accidentally while on a date. It might happen this way. . . .

You are sitting with your sweetheart on the couch. You had planned to take in a movie, but after her parents go out for the evening, she suddenly suggests that you stay inside. She picks up a book of love poetry and wonders what you think of a certain poem by Tennyson. You lean over to read the poem. Suddenly you are sitting right next to her. The poem is entitled "Kisses." You look down at the page and begin:

> *Once he drew*
> *With one long kiss my whole soul through*
> *My lips, as the sunlight drinketh dew.*

You are just about to kiss her when she takes the initiative by moving forward to kiss you. What a pleasant surprise!

You yield to her, becoming passive for a moment as she leads the way. You are so torpid, so easy, so yielding that as she presses her mouth against yours, your lips slowly part and her tongue slips inside your mouth for a moment. Now she is perhaps a bit shocked, and she draws back.

"We better stop for a while," she says.

"No, no."

Now you kiss her, and as you do her lips open and your tongue slides lightly and effortlessly into the soft interior of her mouth. You can hear her breathing. You have forgotten to breathe yourself. Finally you remember to inhale through your nose so that you can prolong the kiss. Your heart is pounding and you feel you have broken through to new territory—and indeed you have. You think you have been perhaps too aggressive. But your fears are allayed when you feel her tongue meet yours. Her mouth feels and tastes so delicious as your tongues twist about each other. And now her tongue pushes slowly and deeply into your mouth. She is so bold, almost brazen in her exploration.

There are no words that can adequately describe the sensation of the French kiss. Suffice it to say that you have now reached an advanced stage of kissing that can lead to almost symbiotic closeness with your lover. Handle this kiss with care and it will pay you rich dividends. You and your lover will get to know each other in a new and intimate way, for the French kiss can bring you closer together than even the act of sex.

Her family was expected back in two hours. Can you believe it, here they come now! How can it be? Have two hours slipped by so quickly? Your heart is still beating fast as the two of you move slightly apart. But you feel that you are still in contact with her. Somehow the French kiss has brought you so close together that for hours and days afterward you will feel different toward each other. It's as if a mystical connection links the two of you together. Ah, the delight of it! Ah, the secret thrill!

Do you like French kissing?

Ninety-nine percent of men and women said they liked this kiss at least some of the time, making it one of the most popular forms of kissing.

WOMEN:
"When I think of French kissing, one man in particular comes to mind. His French kisses weren't sloppy or overly wet. They were penetrating. He used to play chase with his tongue and my tongue in such a way that I wanted it to never stop."

"Very much—you feel like you're melting into each other."

"I like the speed, depth, unification with the other."

MEN:
"The more tongue the better!"

"I like deep, fast, hard tongue kisses."

"The French kiss I could do for hours. I place one hand on the girl's lower back and the other by the side of her head and play with her hair. I breathe with my nose and playfully stick my tongue in and out of her mouth, licking her lips and sucking the air out of her mouth."

"I don't enjoy wide-open wet exploring. I like to French with the mouth only slightly open and prefer a softer, more gently probing kiss."

"When I was first kissed this way, I felt, in some sense, violated. I didn't want anybody putting anything of theirs in anything of mine! If I'd been asked, I would've been more receptive; but I wasn't, and it seemed a bit gross. After a few times, and some weeks, I got the hang of it, but it's not my favorite form. I do enjoy having someone run her tongue along the sides of my teeth, up around the gums. I don't enjoy the stabbing, penetrating, rigid-tongued kiss. I like the fooling-around kind of kiss; a little dance kind of kissing."

Women's advice for men

Many women said that although they liked the French kiss, they found that men resorted to it too often, were too unimaginative (didn't move their tongues enough), or were too aggressive (initiating French kissing too early in a relationship). Their advice for men: (1) go slower, (2) don't French on the first—or even the second or third—date, (3) be gentle, (4) try to sense your partner's mood and respond in kind.

"Men seem not to know any other way to kiss. It can be okay at times, but not *every* time."

"I don't like a lot of tongue. I really hate kissing someone for the first time and having their tongue go down my throat."

"DON'T FISH-MOUTH! Some guys feel like they have to completely overtake your mouth with theirs . . . yeech! And *listen* to your partner. If they're kissing you in a certain way, chances are that's how they want to be kissed back."

"Slow down! Your tongue doesn't have to dart furiously in and out of my mouth. Take your time, tease a bit, let me get my tongue in your mouth once in a while."

"Don't shove your tongue into your girlfriend's mouth too quickly, and don't go too deep."

"I like French kissing if it's soft, sensual, and intimate; as long as it's not slobbering or deep throat. Gentle, delicate French kisses deepen intimacy."

"I like it but not when I feel suffocated by the person's tongue. I like light French kissing."

"Sometimes it's invasive if you're not in a serious or long-time relationship."

"If the other person just wiggles his tongue it's no good. There needs to be passion and sensuality. I hate being sucked or swallowed by kissing."

Men's advice for women

"Put more passion into your French kisses. Touch me with your hands if they are free."

"Don't use your tongue as a DART!"

"Take things slowly. Let the kiss expand into a French kiss *if* it can. Sometimes it just is not appropriate."

"Just get into it and breathe through your nose if you have to, or breathe through the corner of your mouth."

"Enjoy the sensitivity, the intimacy. Slow and steady! Our tongues don't have to *fight!*"

Other comments

One woman told us that she thought her mouth was unraveling the first time her boyfriend's tongue entered her mouth. She couldn't believe what she was feeling. It was so sensual, so intimate, so expressive.

Many people reported that French kissing was their favorite type of kiss. One enthusiast said that she does tongue exercises so that she can French kiss for longer periods of time. She actually trains for it like an athlete. A good exercise is eating mashed potatoes, she claims, because they have the texture and consistency of the inside of someone's mouth.

Another woman said, "The most challenging things are how to get someone to allow you to show them how to kiss (nobody wants to be told they don't know how!) and how to get some finesse into Frenching."

Why is it called the "French" kiss?

The term *French kiss* came into the English language in 1923 as a slur on the French culture, which was thought to be overly concerned with sexual matters. In France it's not called a French kiss; it's called a tongue kiss or soul kissing.

Is there anything you don't like about French kissing?

WOMEN:

"I don't like the fact that some guys misinterpret it as leading further. I see French kissing as just a normal part of kissing, but a lot of men think I'm overly forward and that tongues involved means groping is allowed as well."

"When it's sloppy and really wet."

"I do not like when saliva gets all over my face."

MEN:

"I don't like it when *all* a woman wants to do is French kiss. What about some variation, some soft kisses?"

"Unshared garlic . . . if she has had some and I haven't—ouch!"

"Tongue-gagging, wide-mouth, slobbering kisses. Yuk!"

Licking tongues

The essence of French kissing is tongue contact. And one of the most basic kinds of tongue contact is licking. With this in mind, we asked people what they thought about the subject. Their responses form probably the most comprehensive discussion of licking ever compiled.

Did you ever lick your partner's tongue? What was this like? Do you have any suggestions for how to enjoy this type of kiss?

MEN:

"It's a requirement to get to the more deeply intimate forms of kissing! Everyone literally does it differently, from slow, languid tongue massages, to fast-and-furious tongue tangles. If it's the first time, go slowly and really feel the sensations. Run circles around her lips (where yours meet), then around her tongue. For something different, go for the gum-cleft in front . . . or tickle the roof of her mouth (very ticklish there)."

"Yes, it feels very smooth and good. Let your tongue search out hers."

"I've done it and the tongue felt nice and smooth . . . until I got to the top of the tongue. Then it felt quite rough. To enjoy this kiss, stay to the sides of the other person's tongue."

"What I like about licking her tongue is the intimacy of being so close to someone."

"It can be nice to lick her tongue, but you have to know your partner very well to be comfortable with it. And it helps for her to be quite relaxed."

"Dueling tongues is one of the most pleasurable parts of kissing. I like to examine all the parts of my partner's mouth with my tongue and have her do the same with mine."

"Licking your partner's tongue feels great! My only suggestion is, don't let the feel of her tongue bother you."

"Take it easy and make sure the kiss is balanced. This type of kiss is very enjoyable but not if one partner is down the other's throat and the *quiet* partner feels overpowered. You need to work carefully, approach slowly, and stay in control. Frequent stopping to swallow saliva and to catch one's breath is also advisable. Being somewhat evasive adds to the fun—i.e. quickly licking your partner's tongue and backing off to wait for a response."

WOMEN:
"I'm assuming you don't mean directly licking someone's tongue, as in they stick out their tongue and you lick it. I don't see the point. If you mean French kissing, well then, sure! And it's great once you and your partner figure out each other's rhythms and techniques. For people to whom this may sound gross, I suggest keeping an open mind (as in everything) and try it. They'll never say no again."

"I have licked my lover's tongue. It was slippery, but also had tiny bumps."

"I like licking his tongue. I think people will either enjoy it or not. I suppose that one might learn to like it if one practices learning to enjoy it at a comfortable rate."

"Great French kissing requires a certain amount of licking. The thing to do is relax and don't think your tongue has to be a plunger or anything. Start slowly or your partner will feel like you're eating them, not kissing them."

Advanced French Kissing

Each of these variations was suggested by some creative soul who responded to the Internet kissing survey:

- Twist your tongue around hers.
- Wrestle with her tongue.
- Playfully lick the very tip of her tongue.
- Tell her to stick out her tongue, then lick it.
- Repeatedly lick her tongue while it's still in her mouth.
- Lick the top of her mouth.
- Gently, then vigorously, suck her tongue.
- Chew her tongue with your teeth.
- Explore her teeth and gums with your tongue as if you were searching for something.

Variations on the basic French kiss

What specific techniques do you use in French kisses? What subtle variations have you experienced in tongue contact during French kisses?

WOMEN:
"Hmmmm . . . well, attempting tongue acrobatics usually doesn't work. I think starting slowly and not just shoving your tongue down someone's throat works best. Again, it's all in discovering a mutual rhythm. And not necessarily having lip contact while you French kiss is good, too."

"Variations: Rolling your tongue around the other's; exploring the roof of their mouth or their teeth; using your tongue to get the other's lip; and tongue wrestling."

"There are tons of variation—gentle slow darting tongues that lick your lips and then move into your mouth, twining tongues, sucking tongues. . . . Some people are really aggressive and you just take a submissive role and let them probe your mouth. Other times you're aggressive and lead all the tongue play. It can be really playful, sensuous, passionate, anything at all."

"I love to tongue wrestle. I have had him bite down on my tongue slightly as I am working it in and out. And of course I return the favor."

MEN:
"Twisting my tongue around hers and playing with the sides of a woman's tongue, and, yes, licking the top of her mouth with my tongue—gets 'em every time! Some women have tried to play with the tip of my tongue and I like that."

"I like to take the tongue and suck it into my mouth."

"I just sort of walk my tongue around, licking her tongue, her teeth."

"My mouth is open only very slightly, and my tongue is not inserted very far."

"Gentle fluttering of the tongue . . . circling . . . slow gentle movements . . . no darting for the back of the throat."

"I just move my tongue around a lot, which works okay for me. I like the twirling-tongue-around-the-mouth technique."

"Move slowly. Alternate keeping your tongue firm and really soft. Pay attention to the tip of your partner's tongue, play with it. Lubricate lips from the inside. Light rubbing is exciting! Extended French kissing might require ingenious ways of saliva disposal."

Do's and don'ts of French kissing

A young man from France recently complained that Americans don't know how to tongue kiss properly. He said they were too passive, and that in France, lovers really roll their tongues around and around and are much more active. But being passive at times is a key element of French kissing. The following basic pointers should help you perfect your own creative French kissing style and make you immune to criticism even from natives of France.

Do:
- Take an active part in the kiss. Push your tongue into your partner's mouth. It may feel funny at first, but you'll get over your shyness in no time.
- Take a passive part at times. When your partner pushes his or her tongue into your mouth, relax and enjoy the sensation, meeting him or her with your tongue.
- Breathe through your nose so that you can prolong the kiss.
- Close your eyes now and then so that you can concentrate on the feelings.
- Utter little inarticulate cries and moans to communicate some of your excitement to your partner.
- Explore the roof of your partner's mouth, as well as the inside of the cheeks, the teeth, the region under the tongue, and the palatoglossal arch at the side of the back of the mouth. Your main interest, of course, will be your

partner's tongue because it will feel so sinfully soft and will respond to your every move and touch.

DON'T:
- Don't be afraid of tongue contact. Some lovers get shy when they encounter their partner's tongue. You must overcome this bashfulness.
- Don't press your lips together tightly, because this makes the French kiss impossible.
- Don't gag.
- Don't get nervous if you feel your head swimming and your nerves tingling. It happens to the most experienced lovers during the French kiss.
- Don't chew gum. Gum will only interfere with the kiss and with the sensations you will feel. Besides, gum doesn't feel as good as the inside of your lover's mouth, does it? If you do this kiss properly, with an empty mouth, you'll feel that your soul is merging with your lover's soul. Would you want to spoil that sensation with a wad of chewing gum?
- Don't overdo it. Many people report that they like French kissing so much that they do it for an hour or more nonstop. But, as with anything else, too much of a good thing can be counterproductive. If you tongue-kiss for an hour without stopping you're bound to decrease your pleasure. The solution is to take a short break every five or ten minutes. Chat with your partner. You might talk about the kiss itself. Have a glass of water or some candy. There's nothing like a French kiss between a peppermint-flavored tongue and a cherry Life Saver-flavored mouth! As you can see, the combinations are endless.

The
$\mathcal{E}$SKIMO KISS

Three teenage girls are chatting in the freezing cold evening outside a small wooden bakery in Barrow, Alaska. The sign over the door says DONUTS AND COFFEE. A boy rides up, drops his bicycle in the snow, and goes into the building with one of the girls. As soon as they enter they stand toe-to-toe and begin to rub noses.

A good-looking young woman sets out from the village of Igloolik for a day of seal hunting in the Canadian Arctic, climbing into a small motorboat with her baby strapped to her back. She turns to smile at her husband, who has trudged through the snow to see her off. As she starts the motor, he leans forward and they press their noses to-gether.

The wedding is over, and the newlyweds turn to each other. Ritual drums echo across Canada's Great Slave Lake in the dusky mist as the two lovers rub noses in a prolonged embrace.

These vignettes illustrate an important but little-understood custom known as the Eskimo or nose-rubbing kiss. The kiss is popular not only throughout the Arctic regions, but also among the Maoris of New Zealand, the Society and Sandwich Islanders, the Tongans, and most of the

Malayan races (which is why it is alternately known as the Malay kiss). The kiss is also practiced in Africa and is the predominant form of kissing in Asia. Actually the kiss involves more than simply rubbing noses, as the following instructions demonstrate:

How to do the Eskimo kiss

1. Begin to embrace your partner.
2. Simultaneously bring your faces close.
3. Aim your nose slightly to one side of your lover's nose.
4. When your noses make contact, let them slide along each other.
5. As soon as the tip of your nose reaches your partner's cheek, breathe in through your nose, savoring the fragrance of your lover as you do.
6. Lower your eyelids.
7. Smack your lips in a kissing gesture, but don't actually kiss your partner's cheeks; instead kiss air.
8. Inhale through your mouth as you kiss the air, enjoying the delicious perfume of your lover.
9. Move your nose back and forth slightly, sliding it along the side of your lover's nose.
10. Now and then bump the *tips* of your noses together. Smile and gaze into your lover's eyes while you do this.
11. Occasionally bump the *sides* of your noses together as a variation on the sliding motion that predominates in the kiss.

Variations on the Eskimo kiss

A number of variations on the basic Eskimo kiss have been noted by anthropologists. Darwin described a Malay kiss in which the initiator of the kiss places his or her nose at right angles on the nose of the partner and then rubs it, the entire kiss lasting no longer than a handshake. Cook described a South Sea Islands variety as a brisk mutual rubbing with the end of the nose. Still others have described an Australian variety which consists merely of face rubbing. In many tribes the lover simply pushes his or her mouth and nose against the partner's cheek and then inhales.

Do you ever simply press your face into your lover's as a short interlude of rest between kisses?

"Yes, but not directly nose to nose—more of a nuzzling on the side of their face."

"Yes, usually I press my forehead against some part of their face."

Kissing Tip

Although many men and women consider it childish on an intellectual level, more than 95 percent of them occasionally like to rub noses while kissing.

Do you ever rub noses?
WOMEN:
"Yes, a little now and again."

"Yes, it's hard not to."

"Only with a child. It seems like a childish thing to do."

"I used to when I was a kid. We thought it was funny."

"I don't really care for it, but I've done it."

MEN:

"Definitely. Nose rubbing is loads of fun, alone or with smooches!"

"I like to *bump* noses."

"Rubbing noses works best when you simply want to hug her and keep your faces close."

The
JAPANESE KISS

Recently I visited a radio station to talk about kissing in front of a live in-studio audience. The deejay wanted to demonstrate one of the kisses on the air with two audience members, but suddenly everyone in the studio got very shy. In order to coax a guy and girl up to the front of the stage for a demonstration, I told them about the Japanese kiss.

The Japanese, who are generally very discreet in their personal habits, are rather shy about kissing. They don't really like the custom. They don't even like to talk about the subject.

One young woman from Japan said, "Since coming to America, I have tried to learn American customs, including kissing. I said to my husband, 'Why don't we try to become more like Americans and kiss more?' He got indignant and refused. 'I'm Japanese,' he said, 'not American.' So we don't kiss much. Back in Japan my mother would drop dead if she saw two people kissing in public—really no one kisses in public. She'll immediately turn off the television if the actors kiss."

Here's what I asked the volunteers to do at the radio station (both of them later told me they loved it):

How to do the Japanese kiss

1. Be shy about kissing.
2. Forget what you already know about it.
3. Ignore everything in this book.
4. Stand at least a foot away from your lover.
5. Lean forward.
6. Don't hug or embrace.
7. Don't use your hands at all.
8. Gently touch your closed lips to the lower lip of your lover.
9. Don't say anything.
10. Don't laugh.
11. Be very serious.
12. Act slightly embarrassed about the whole thing.
13. Keep your lips pressed to your partner's for a while, but don't expect any reaction and don't expect to be kissed back.
14. Break off and step back.
15. Be discreet and say nothing about the kiss.

"What good is the Japanese kiss?" I can hear some readers asking themselves. "It's so . . . *sexless!*"

Far from it! Strange as it may seem, the Japanese kiss is one of the most erotic kisses in the book. The element of holding back, of hesitancy, of Taoist simplicity—all this has its arousing effect. After you've been kissing for a number of years you're liable to become jaded. Nothing seems new anymore. Kissing loses its zing, its excitement, its stimulating qualities. But this is largely because you have been trying always to progress, when instead perhaps it is time to regress, to forget, to become the neophyte for a while . . . and kiss as the Japanese do.

$\mathcal{E}$UROPEAN KISSES

The beauty of the Internet is that it gives you immediate access to the world, but sometimes what you hear can be a little insulting. A twenty-three-year-old man from Madrid told me via e-mail, "Although my experience is completely European, I bet we're better kissers than you Americans! Too much Coca-Cola and hamburgers can't be good!"

I kept hearing this same message over and over. Europeans are great kissers, especially those from southern Europe—Spain, France, Italy, Portugal, Greece. It makes you want to travel . . . and kiss.

The bottom line, I discovered, is that Europeans may indeed have the edge when it comes to kissing. But why? A twenty-four-year-old man from Athens, Greece, may have hit on the answer: "They're much more open to it, in conformity with the much more liberated attitude of Europeans toward personal relations. America is very much a country where public taboos and puritanism dominate society."

Feeling a little defensive about being an American, I set out to discover all I could about the differences between those sexy Europeans and the rest of us.

Do Europeans kiss differently than Americans?

WOMEN:

"Yes. In my experience, they aren't as hung up about French kissing. French kissing is considered pretty normal."

"I don't know about Europeans, but Israelis and Canadians do. The Israeli and the Canadian that I dated were just more in tune with women. Americans have this complex of getting right to the goal (i.e., sex and orgasm) and don't take the time to appreciate what it takes to get there. The Israeli and the Canadian were very self-confident, and wanted to please their partner as much as themselves. Americans could use a lesson or two."

Have you ever kissed anyone who was a native of a European country? If so, what country were they from? Who did you kiss and what was the kiss like?

WOMEN:

"My German boyfriend was an excellent kisser; a friend from England was not so great; an old boyfriend from Belgium was decent."

"I am twenty-three years old and female. I live in the United States, but I am a French citizen. I have been in the U.S. for two years now. The Europeans I kissed were from France, the Netherlands, and Scotland. They were students, with good education, upper class and—males!!! *What was the kiss like?* France—great! Well, you've heard of the French kiss. The first guy I kissed was French so I am used to it! The Netherlands—about the same as far as I remember, but with less creativity in the kiss than the French; very *classic* in the standards, no deviation! Scotland—like the Dutch one, very basic, but still good! The United States—just in case you want to have a European opinion . . . well, it sure was different from the European kisses. I don't want to go too *deep* in the details, but there were a lot of kisses in the mouth (with a lot of creativity). Europeans tend to kiss in different places more than the Americans. I think French people are proud of their reputation as lovers and I also think that the reputation is kind of true. We are obsessed by love and we *want* to live up to that reputation. This gets us moving and creating."

"I'm twenty and from California. I kissed several people from the U.K.—mostly drunken, sloppy kisses. Two sober men in the U.K.—nice, tender kisses, quite gentle really. A German, my boyfriend, had fairly sloppy kisses, and was very passionate. He can be very tender at times as well, but that is not his usual style. Joe from Turkey gave friendly sweet kisses that were just for fun, and we both knew it. A lot of tongue, but not all the way down my throat, which was nice."

Advice for men

If you'd like to develop a sexy European flair for kissing, here are some suggestions from your cousins on the continent.

- Try to be more in tune with your girlfriend.
- Don't rush on to having sex. Linger over kissing.
- Please her as much as you please yourself.
- Go easy—don't choke her with your tongue in French kissing. Don't viciously jab it into her mouth.
- Stop slobbering over her when Frenching.
- For heaven's sake, swallow your own spit!
- Be more attentive to her and stroke her gently while kissing.

"I'm thirty and from Scotland. I've kissed women from Scotland and England. The most recent one was too aggressive and used far too much tongue. Previous ones have been gentle, soft, infinitely fascinating."

"I've kissed several women from England who were great kissers, and a few French women—one great, the rest okay."

"I kissed an Italian woman and she was good at it."

"I'm twenty-one and a native of France. French girls kiss with lust, love, and perfection. English girls are a little bit cold when kissing. German girls a bit hard and animalistic."

"I am a twenty-five-year-old male from Lisbon, Portugal. We kiss our friends in the face when we meet. Only men shake hands. Regarding romantic kisses, I have kissed Portuguese women. Some of them know how to kiss, others don't, but most do."

"I'm twenty-three and from Spain. Friendly kisses: in Spain, that's the way we say hello between a man and woman, and the way we say goodbye, and the way we say happy birthday, and the way we say Merry Christmas, and so on. We kiss twice on the cheeks. (In France, they give three. In Germany and Switzerland, nothing at all.)"

In your opinion, do Europeans kiss any differently than Americans? What specific differences have you noticed?

WOMEN:
"In Italy, kissing friends and business acquaintances is a common form of greeting that wouldn't happen in England, Ireland, or the U.S."

"Greeting kisses are very different in Europe. The Belgians kiss cheeks (that is, smack lips in the air while pressing cheeks together) four times with family members, three times with friends."

"I'm twenty-seven and from Virginia and have traveled extensively. Europeans are better kissers. European French kisses are not as wet as American ones. U.S. men tend to slobber—yuck!"

MEN:
"Here's how I see it. I'm twenty-six and from Austria and I've traveled all throughout Europe and have kissed girls in various countries:

Portugal	➡	shy, shy
Italy	➡	quite emancipated
Belgium	➡	maybe the best
Germany	➡	freethinking and lustful
France	➡	bad breath
England	➡	wild things

"I think American girls—at least those I met—are more shy than the European girls. This includes kissing in public, too. American girls usually need a romantic environment to get in the mood. But after that I'd say there's no difference except one—but maybe my samples (sorry for the word) were not so statistically significant: American girls don't open their mouths as wide as the girls from southern Europe."

"I'm not sure about this because I didn't kiss so many American girls. I am thirty-two and from the Netherlands. But Americans seem not able to really lose themselves in a kiss. They're a little boring."

"I find Americans and British to be fairly reticent when it comes to kissing, and the Europeans to be fairly open. Being from England, however, I do not see myself as typically British in this regard."

What is your experience kissing Europeans? Are they good kissers? If so, why? What, if anything, do they do differently?

WOMEN:

A twenty-six-year-old from Norway said, "British people always kiss you on the cheek if you try to welcome them with a hug. I don't like it. Firstly, because it reduces the amount of skin contact, secondly because I feel like drying my cheek afterwards, and thirdly because I worry about my makeup."

"European men are great kissers; they linger longer than Americans, who tend to rush kisses to move on."

A twenty-two-year-old from Ireland said, "Yes, they are more attentive to you; they stroke more gently, and don't plunge their tongues like most men in the city where I live."

"I have tried it with only one boy, but he is really good," said a twenty-two-year-old from Sweden. "Not only his mouth, but his whole body shows me that he loves me. We have found out and taught each other how we prefer it. I think that the most important thing is to learn together."

"In my experience, Europeans are a lot less sloppy than Americans (less saliva)."

MEN:

A twenty-one-year-old from France said, "Europeans kiss as well as Brazilians and Latin Americans, and they kiss better than Americans (who are too shy, too official)."

A nineteen-year-old from England said, "Couldn't compare, really. (I must say that my U.S.-kiss was a bit 'violent,' but that could have been the drink kissing.)"

A twenty-three-year-old from Spain said, "Of course we're good kissers! I think it depends more on age than on nationality. And I think it's the man who's the one imposing his way of kissing, so I can't tell too much (unless she's so hot that she overwhelms you)."

Are there different kissing customs that you noticed in any European country?

WOMEN:

"In Greece, men don't automatically try to kiss you on the first couple of dates. American men, on the other hand, seem to want *everything* on the first date."

"French and Italian men tend to greet you by kissing you on each cheek."

"An old boyfriend from Brussels would greet me with a kiss on each of my cheeks."

"In the U.K. people *snog* a lot. The definition of snog is not completely agreed on by everyone, but my experience is that it involves kissing with tongue, most often between people who are not seriously involved. It often occurs when drunk, and among U.K. university girls in particular, it seems that an evening at a disco can hardly be complete without snogging someone, in other words *pulling,* though pulling can also imply spending the night with the person."

"The French have a habit of always kissing everyone on each cheek at every meeting from new acquaintances to old friends. It's quite amusing to observe the French when they're hanging out at a cafe because there are endless rounds of kissing as people show up. Female/female and male/female—not male/male in my experience. I also noticed increased kissing as a greeting among friends in the U.K. in the '70s, but on the lips it was again only female/female and male/female."

"I'm twenty-seven and from Ireland. The French are very willing to kiss complete strangers when introduced to them. Only the French can understand the complexities of whether to kiss once, twice, or thrice on first meeting."

Are people more open about kissing in public in Europe than in the United States?

WOMEN:
"Yes, definitely on the continent."

"Maybe in France. Certainly not in England or Ireland."

"I'm twenty-two and Swedish. They are more open in Switzerland than in Sweden. Here, in Switzerland where I'm visiting, you often see people trying to get their tongues down to the other's stomach. In Sweden we do deep kissing more in private. In public, only half-deep kisses are considered normal."

"Sure, look at all the Italian men who kiss each other. You don't see many American men doing that! American men think of that as a sign of homosexuality, where European men see it as a sign of friendship."

"Are they ever! It's kind of a social no-no here in the U.S., I think. People don't feel as free to do it."

MEN:
"I'm thirty and from Scotland. Europe is by no means uniform; in general you can divide western Europe into the reserved northern-Saxon types, and the fiery, kiss-happy Mediterranean types. But that's a vast over-generalization of course."

A twenty-seven-year-old from Ireland said, "Yes, Americans seem to be really uptight about the idea."

"I'm twenty-two and from Belgium. Over here we don't make any fuss about kissing in public. Some girls, even boys, are more reserved in public, but I think that's personal. On the other hand one does occasionally see a couple of lovebirds on a bench in the park kiss each other. People aren't shocked by something like that."

Do you recall seeing people kiss in public in any European country? Where?

Replies from all over Europe mentioned France more often than any other country. A twenty-eight-year-old from Paris said, "In France it is common practice. But I don't remember seeing it as much in other countries." Other countries where there is a lot of public kissing include Greece, Italy, Belgium, and all over in Denmark (according to a twenty-one-year-old male from Copenhagen). Said a twenty-seven-year-old male from Ireland, "Yes, every country I have visited (England, Wales, France, Luxembourg, Denmark, Sweden, Russia), especially France, Sweden, and Denmark. In Scandinavia, it is much more common in the summer to see couples kissing in public, but if you have seen the weather, you'll understand why." A twenty-six-year-old Austrian male who traveled all over Europe observed, "The only country where I did not see people kissing in public was Turkey."

A twenty-three-year-old fellow in Madrid reported, "Of course in Spain: at night, it's everywhere. And in France."

How to kiss like a European

After reading all this criticism, Americans and others around the world may wonder what they can do to catch up with European lovers, especially those from southern Europe who seem to be having so much fun with kissing. Here's a summary of the advice and criticisms from the Internet survey. Rest assured that with a little practice, you too will be kissing just like those sexy Europeans:

Advice for men and women

- Give your lover a series of hello kisses.
- Kiss a number of times when parting.
- Stand closer to your lover during a kiss.
- Try to maintain a more liberal attitude toward sex in general.
- Kiss for the sake of kissing.
- Think of French kissing as normal.
- Kiss in public more openly.
- Lose yourself in your kisses.
- Enjoy yourself, but remember to please your partner, too.

The

TROBRIAND ISLANDS

KISS

Here's a kiss your lover has probably never heard of—a kiss named after the South Sea Islands where it's so commonplace that everyone does it. The kiss was unknown in the rest of the world until 1929 when anthropologist Bronislaw Malinowski visited the Trobriand Islands (pronounced: TROW-bree-ahnd), investigated their bizarre sexual customs, and wrote a marvelous account of his research, *The Sexual Life of Savages*.

The Trobriand Islands are located about 1,850 miles due north of Sydney, Australia, in that part of the South Pacific Ocean known as the Solomon Sea. Natives of the islands are dark-skinned and belong to the Paupo-Melanesian race. Malinowski studied every aspect of their sexual life, from premarital intercourse to marriage to pregnancy and childbirth to lovemaking and the erotic life. His research is highly respected, and his work ranks close to Darwin's in the realm of cultural studies.

Malinowski found that the Trobriand natives consider our custom of kissing (pressing lips to lips) a rather silly and dull practice. But although they don't kiss as we define kissing, they do use the mouth during lovemaking. Two lovers will typically begin by talking for a long time, grooming each other's hair, and hugging and caressing each other. Then they rub noses just like the Eskimos. They also rub their *cheeks* together and they rub mouth against mouth—without kissing. Next they suck each other's tongues in a sort of variation on the French kiss. When things heat up, they begin to rub tongue against tongue. Next—and this is the crucial step—they bite and suck each other's lower lip until the lip bleeds, and then they bite off each other's eyelashes. This biting off of eyelashes is done during orgasm as well as during the earlier parts of love-making. They also exchange saliva from mouth to mouth and bite each other's chin, cheeks, and nose. During more intense moments they also pull so forcefully on each other's hair that they often tear handfuls of it right from their lover's head! Such is the nature of kissing among the Trobriand Islanders.

For those brave souls willing to try something new, the instructions for the Trobriand Islands kiss follow. You needn't do each and every step. Skip around and try whichever ones interest you.

How to do the Trobriand Islands kiss

1. Begin by getting close. Sit on a mat together.
2. Have a conversation.
3. Hug and caress.
4. Run your hands through your lover's hair.
5. Rub noses.
6. Rub cheek against cheek.
7. Rub your mouths together—without kissing!
8. Suck each other's tongues.
9. *Rub* tongue against tongue.
10. Suck your lover's lower lip *vigorously*.

11. Bite your lover's lower lip until it bleeds.
12. Exchange saliva from mouth to mouth.
13. Bite your partner's chin.
14. Bite your partner's cheek.
15. Nip at your partner's nose with your teeth.
16. Thrust your hands into your partner's hair and pull forcefully.
17. Bite off your lover's eyelashes.

Probably the most unusual part of the kiss is the biting of the eyelashes. (According to Malinowski, everyone in the Trobriand Islands has eyelashes that are bitten short.) But other aspects of the kiss are not unfamiliar. For example, many Westerners like to pull each other's hair, rub noses, and even suck and bite their lover's lower lip. When I asked people whether they ever sucked their partner's lower lip, 87 percent said yes—which suggests that your lover may be amenable to trying some aspects of the Trobriand Islands kiss.

The Trobriand Islands kiss requires a wild and uninhibited nature. Practicing it may change you completely; but if you feel experimental, go ahead and set the ritual in motion. Let the savage in you free. Make tribal drums beat. And when your friends ask what happened to your eyelashes, simply smile and say, "Haven't you heard of the Trobriand Islands kiss?"

PART FOUR

Kissing Technique

$\mathcal{K}$ISSING TECHNIQUE

A young college woman was dating a fellow who was a very good kisser. One night they were French kissing in her dorm when she suddenly sat back.

"I know this will sound crazy," she said, "but am I . . . well . . . am I *doing* it right?"

As she recalls, he proceeded to spend the next several hours showing her how to kiss better and enjoy it more, teaching her in particular how to be more aggressive with her tongue. Ah, if only all lessons and homework were like this! Without further delay, then, let's begin our course in contemporary kissing techniques.

To look or not to look

The question of whether lovers should kiss with their eyes open or closed is of fundamental importance. It was the question that prompted me to write this book, and I'm glad to be able to report some definitive answers here. More than two-thirds of those surveyed preferred to keep their eyes closed while kissing, but didn't mind if their partner kept his or hers open. Only one in three like to kiss with eyes open—and if *your* lover does, you can take it as a compliment. "I prefer kissing with my eyes open unless the girl isn't that pretty," said one twenty-four-year-old.

But you shouldn't worry about your appearance. If your partner kisses with his or her eyes open, everything will look out of focus. Indeed, because the brain interprets nearby faces as erotic, you'll actually appear sexier to your lover when you're mouth to mouth. So open your eyes, too, occasionally and enjoy the thrill!

"I like to see what my lover looks like and how he's responding."

"Sometimes the effect of prolonged eye contact is amazing."

"I like eyes open if I'm in love. I like to see my lover's eyes. It makes me feel connected soulfully to him."

"I usually kiss with my eyes closed because it's more romantic. But sometimes I like to peek at my husband, because his expression is so tender."

"I enjoy watching my boyfriend and me kiss. With my eyes open I'll turn my head to look in a mirror. It's quite a turn-on."

Talking while kissing

Silent lovers, listen to this! The majority of men and women (68 percent) enjoyed talking while kissing. "Not while actually applying both lips to her, but in between," said one man. "I tend to compliment her or talk about sex." A thirty-four-year-old woman who lives in Bucharest, Romania, said, "I poke fun at my partner and make dirty remarks."

Of course it's difficult to carry on a serious conversation

while kissing intently. Said one woman from Ottawa, Canada, "With my lover we carry on conversations between kisses, and as the kissing gets more passionate the talking slows down or stops and goes from metaphysical topics to endearments." A twenty-one-year-old woman respondent said, "Sometimes we just talk about kissing."

The technique of talking while kissing is rather easy to master. Simply interrupt the kiss and, while still embracing your lover, say something nice. Then go back to the kiss.

Kissing Tip

For talking and kissing, try the Chico Marx technique. When replying to his wife, who caught him kissing a chorus girl, he said, "I wasn't kissing her. I was whispering in her mouth."

Although most Westerners consider sex words taboo, about one in three couples use sexually charged or coarse language during kissing. One woman frankly admitted, "No, I have a problem with this and can't do it because of my Catholic upbringing." But those who talk dirty report that it's a turn-on to occasionally whisper something sexy to their partner between kisses. Sometimes such a comment will even get a laugh, which brings us to:

Laughing while kissing

If your partner laughs or giggles while kissing, don't get insulted. Sexual intimacy produces laughter in many people. Indeed, 87 percent of men and 98 percent of women reported that they sometimes giggled when kissing because of the pleasure they felt. And 2 percent even cried when a kiss felt too good to bear. So if your partner laughs while kissing, you know you're doing something *right*.

What to do with your hands while kissing

The initial contact between lovers is usually lip to lip; the hands may not even play a part in lovemaking until after the initial kisses. A man often likes a woman to cup his face in her hands while kissing him. It's a very tender and loving gesture. A woman may enjoy having a man run his fingers or hands up and down her spine. Here are some other suggestions:

WOMEN:
"I gently caress the back of his neck or his cheeks or run my fingers through his hair."

"I play with his hair, massage his muscles, pull his shirt out so I can feel the skin on his back."

"My hands are always moving—through his hair and over his back. Sometimes we clasp hands or a hand. My fingers touch his face (eyes, cheek, forehead, lips). My hands cup his ears. I also place my hands on his hips."

"If it's my husband, I'll touch his hair, his ears, his shoulders, back, buttocks, etc."

"I stroke the other person's head, arms, and body."

"I like to hold his face, rub his shoulders, rub his chest, and sometimes rub his leg."

"I explore his body, gently. Tease."

MEN:

"I usually rub her ass, upper leg, thigh, sides of breasts, ears, or even fingers."

"I usually put my hands around the girl's waist."

Telephone kisses

Generally a favorite with kids, telephone kisses now and then find their way into the phone conversations of lovers. The technique simply involves making a kissing sound into your phone's receiver, usually before you hang up. Some people say they feel childish doing it, so you'll have to judge for yourself whether it's something you want to try. (When I asked in the Internet survey, "Do you ever kiss over the phone? How do you accomplish this?" a young man from Madrid, Spain, replied, "No. What kind of phones have you got in the U.S.A.?")

MEN:

"I make a smooch sound over the phone. Just smack over the mouthpiece."

"Just a smooch now and then. Most of the time, verbal romance via the phone makes me feel awkward."

"No. It sounds stupid and makes the receiver all juicy."

WOMEN:

"I love nice juicy phone kisses. I have a phone friend who I met on the phone from a wrong number. He calls and kisses me without even saying hello. I love it."

"I do it all the time."

"Yes, I explain to whomever exactly how I am going to kiss them when I get them alone."

"My daughter and I have developed our own kiss to each other. It starts off with an *mmm* sound which is extended into a smack by saying *mmm-uuuu*—it's a verbal kiss."

"I see my boyfriend only on weekends (he lives fifty miles away), and we talk on the phone every night, so we'll often end our conversations with a kiss over the phone."

"Yes. I say, 'Close your eyes. Think of me, take a very deep breath, and let's kiss!'"

When to kiss on a date

In the first edition of this book I mentioned a young woman I had heard about who didn't kiss boys until the sixth date. Well, I received a letter from another young woman who said my advice was "a little on the conservative side." She went on to say, "I've kissed many, many boys (and men), and I've never waited until the sixth date! And I don't believe there is any specific time during a date that is more or less appropriate for kissing!"

She continued, "Also, try and be more aware of what's going on in the younger generation. You wouldn't believe how oversexed these youngsters are." (By the way, I love getting advice like this. It just opens my eyes right up.) "Visit a New York City nightclub," she advised me. "There are people making out all over, in plain view, hundreds of them. Teenagers go out to *hook up* (meet members of the opposite sex and fool around with them). By fooling around I mean making out. There are also those that will meet someone and go home with them and have sex. I think this is disgusting, but it happens."

Well, I am not going to advise you to wait until the sixth date. I think her advice is sound, and it echoes the replies I've been getting with the latest kissing survey. About 85 percent of men and women now believe it is okay to kiss on a first date, provided you feel comfortable with the person you're dating or if you've known your date for some time.

The thing to remember is that the kiss will come much more easily if you're on the same wavelength as your date before you attempt it. Keep the conversation going, gaze into each other's eyes for long periods of time, and let the excitement mount between you. Someone once said that if you look into anyone's eyes for five minutes you'll fall in love with them. Plenty of eye contact will get you in tune with each other so that the kiss seems like the natural thing to do.

Kissing tip

Here are some ideas for when to kiss on a date:

- When you leave a restaurant and you're standing close together trying to decide where to go.
- When at a museum together and you're close and examining a work of art.
- In the middle of the date after you've had a good conversation and have made eye contact for an extended time.
- After you make some funny joke and you're both laughing together and in a good mood.

The counterkiss

One day I observed two lovers necking on a train. The young woman waited after each kiss before kissing her boyfriend back, gazing dreamily at him for a moment, then leaning forward and kissing him a little lower down on the cheek than he had kissed her. After a while she started peppering him with quick little kisses until he burst out laughing. She was a classic counterkisser.

The counterkiss is a technique rather than a specific kind of kiss. In fact, you can counterkiss with just about any kind of kiss—a French kiss, a wet kiss, a biting kiss, and so on. The object is to wait and see exactly how your lover is kissing you before kissing him or her back. Just as an army can launch various counteroffensives during warfare, you can respond to a kiss with the same general kind of kiss or with a slightly different kind of kiss. Of course, no two kisses are ever exactly alike, but in counterkissing you purposefully become conscious of the type of kiss you are getting so that you can either respond in kind or subtly vary the kiss you have just received. In this way you'll manage to puzzle, amuse, and tantalize your partner and keep your kissing session moving ever forward into fascinating new areas of tactile fun.

The make-up kiss

One of the most delightful thrills of being in love is getting over a quarrel and making up. Throughout the ages lovers have argued over the silliest things, getting angry and vowing never to see each other again. Then inevitably—sometimes within a matter of minutes—they become reconciled, and all their angry emotions are transmuted into the most enraptured devotion; they feel they've never been closer. With your differences ironed out, you'll enjoy a new lease on love. The kiss (known as *Versöhnungskuss* in German) that marks such a turning point celebrates a special and wonderful experiment in the alchemy of the heart.

There is, however, another side to the make-up kiss. Some people feel it is too easy a solution. One twenty-five-year-old woman from Ontario, Canada, says, "I used to kiss and make up. I won't anymore because my feelings about the kisses (usually really good) mix me up and I shove existing anger back inside me. As a result, after the kiss I feel like I've been corked and can't deal with things further." Another perceptive twenty-year-old woman from Chicago says, "If the argument is truly resolved, make-up kisses are the best in the world. If the argument isn't settled, the kiss will let you know."

How to kiss at the movies

Every time I run a kissing survey I find that fewer and fewer people like to kiss at the movies. Currently only about 25 percent of moviegoers neck during a film. They generally don't like to have people sitting behind them when they kiss. And they usually kiss during romantic or tender moments or when the lights first go down. Kisses in a theater aren't too passionate; they're more likely to be short pecks.

If your partner enjoys kissing at the movies, teach him or her the copy-cat game: You kiss whenever the actors do. Of course this works best at romantic films.

WOMEN:
"Generally I don't like doing it when there are people behind me. I've kissed when there are heartwarming scenes, for example, families coming together or beautiful scenes of nature. It's close and warm being next to my boyfriend in a dark and nonintimate setting."

"I don't like to kiss, but I do *love* to grope at the movies, almost to the point of excruciation!"

"Maybe one or two small kisses in a movie. During a romantic or emotional part that we both can relate to."

"I kiss during romantic scenes, and hold hands tightly during scary scenes."

"If a movie doesn't hold my attention, I feel I might as well enjoy something."

MEN:
"For $8.50, I like to see the movie!"

"Love to kiss at the flicks. Tend to sit one third from the front, in the center so we can see. We kiss whenever the fancy strikes."

"It depends on the movie and how much you want to kiss her. A boring movie can make you kiss her immediately. I try not to disturb anyone and sit myself at the back. I hate those heads kissing in the middle of the film. I begin to say something like: 'There's stupid people in the world' or 'Perhaps we should take a walk, 'cause I can't see anything.' "

How to kiss in a car

So many survey respondents (92 percent) said they enjoyed kissing in cars that it's a wonder car manufacturers don't list "plenty of room for kissing" as a feature in their advertising pitch. Here are just a few comments on when, where, and how to do it.

"My boyfriend usually drives, and when the car is moving I generally give him cheek kisses due to the angle. When the car stops at a light he'll turn his face to me and we'll kiss on the lips. Sometimes we've even kissed on the lips while the car is moving, but we do that only when traffic is light."

"When I kiss with a date in a car, it usually takes place in the front seat. It's always fun to watch the windows eventually fog up, too!"

"I like kissing in a car because it is small, and you have to make concessions in order to do what you want. It's fun, too, because silly things usually happen."

"It is very uncomfortable having to contort yourself in a car. Note, I don't like sex in the back seat either. If a male does, I just pass on by him and tell him to grow up!"

"Car kisses are very exciting. The chance that someone will see us kissing adds to the excitement."

"Even though I'm a full-grown adult, there's a certain thrill in this—especially parked on a public street. I think I'm a bit of an exhibitionist!"

How to kiss at parties

Imagine a boy and girl at a party: They're talking to each other when suddenly they notice they're alone in a corner and no one's looking. The excitement has been building between them all evening, and now the moment is right. Quickly they kiss, a stolen kiss, and suddenly a flame ignites in both their hearts, so that even when they wander apart later and talk to other people during the party, they're linked because of that kiss. Such an experience is quite common; in fact, about 80 percent of people like to kiss at parties. Usually they do it off to the side so as not to make a scene.

WOMEN:
"When I kiss at parties I usually give kisses on the cheek or quick pecks on the lips. But if I'm dancing and am physically close to my boyfriend and the music and/or the

moment is romantic, I'll deliver a long-lasting kiss and for a brief moment will sometimes French kiss."

"I like to kiss the men at the party good night with a quick peck on the lips."

"You can sometimes pretend to whisper and give a small kiss in your lover's ear—this can be discreet and exciting."

MEN:
"I always kiss at parties. I look for a private place and . . . to hell with everybody!"

"Kissing at parties in college was fun, but usually around good friends (who were often busy kissing, too), so it was never really a big deal."

"Bathrooms, closets, dark corners on the floor. Borrow a bedroom! Go to the kitchen! Kiss whenever everyone starts getting rude or drunk or bored."

Kissing games

You're never too old for kissing games, and here are some classics that will please lovers of any age:

- *Copy-cat.* In a movie theater or while watching TV, you kiss whenever the actors do.
- *Truth or Dare.* One person at a time is asked embarrassing questions, and if the group votes that he's lying, he has to take a dare, such as giving one of the girls a French kiss.
- *Freeze Tag.* A group of friends runs around the house, and one person is selected to be the freezer, running after the others, attempting to kiss them. When the freezer kisses you, you remain frozen until anyone else unfreezes you with a kiss.

- ***Spin the Bottle.*** One person spins a bottle. If it points to a person of the opposite sex, they kiss in front of the group. In a dark room the game is played with a flashlight instead of a bottle.
- ***Post Office.*** All the girls are out of the room, and an area is partitioned off as a post office, with one boy inside it. One of the other boys tells one of the girls she has some mail. She goes into the post office and is kissed. She exits and the game continues with girls being called in one by one.

Social and business greeting kisses

You've known about social greeting kisses all your life, since they're the type of kiss you give and receive when you're at family gatherings. But not many people realize that the same greeting kiss is becoming increasingly appropriate in some business settings. In fact the larger the city, the more likely business people are to kiss in greeting one another. The custom also tends to be industry specific: people in certain fields—entertainers, consultants, human resources workers, and some health care employees—are more likely to kiss than people in manufacturing, medicine, banking, and accounting. Here are the basic do's and don'ts for the business kiss:

Do:
- Kiss in a business situation only if you feel comfortable doing it and know the person well.
- Kiss at business parties and other social functions, like the annual baseball game, award ceremonies, picnics, or conventions.
- Merely touch cheeks and kiss the air. You could also kiss the person's cheek if you're not wearing lipstick.
- Let your boss initiate the kiss.

DON'T:

- Don't kiss strangers. A kiss on first meeting someone is usually inappropriate.
- Don't kiss in strictly business environments like offices, courts, banks, restaurant meetings, and auditoriums.
- Don't let people kiss you if you feel uncomfortable about it. To avoid a kiss simply stand at arm's length and thrust your hand forward for a handshake.
- Don't kiss directly on the lips.
- Don't smudge your business associate with lipstick; if you're wearing lipstick, simply touch cheeks.
- Don't kiss drunk business associates; they may misinterpret the kiss as a sexual advance.

How to avoid kissing diseases

We'll define a kissing disease as one you can get simply by kissing someone. While this includes infections like the flu, mononucleosis, and more severe things like syphilis and herpes, the good news is that AIDS is not a kissing disease. There are no known cases of AIDS being transmitted by kissing. Levels of the HIV virus in an infected person's saliva are so low that physicians believe there is no danger of getting AIDS by kissing.

You could, however, get mononucleosis from kissing your lover. Mononucleosis, also known as the kissing disease, has become something of a badge of honor for teenagers. With pride they boast to friends and teachers that they can't go to school because they have "mono." The disease is transmitted by kissing (hence the nickname) or by other close personal contact, and it's most common where young people aged between fifteen and twenty-five live together. In colleges and universities the estimated incidence may be as high as 300 to 1,500 cases per 100,000 students. Most people become immune to mono by the time they're forty because they're exposed to a mild form of the disease and develop antibodies. But since there's no way to prevent mono, the best you can do is avoid kissing someone who has it.

With other diseases that can be transmitted through kissing—including flu viruses, herpes, syphilis, etc.—the answer is unfortunately just as vague. One of the chief epidemiologists in the Northeast has said that the best advice the medical profession can give people today about avoiding kissing diseases is simply to use common sense—if you *do* know people who are sick with a communicable disease (for example, if you can see sores on their lips, or you hear them coughing excessively), don't kiss them. There isn't much more you can do. Without a lab test, it's often impossible to know if someone has a communicable disease—the infected person often doesn't know it either. It seems that the medical profession is as advanced on this one as they are on the common cold.

Kissing and drugs

About 90 percent of men and women from around the world prefer to kiss while sober. The small percentage who also enjoy kissing while intoxicated often said they could experience things more fully while sober. Said a thirty-four-year-old woman from Romania, "Both ways have their own perks, but I prefer to do things sober in general." Even fewer (2 percent) said they enjoyed kissing while high on marijuana or other drugs. The consensus seems to be that kissing can provide its own high.

How to talk about kissing

"Everyone should express their kissing needs to their partners, since it can be a fulfilling and bonding experience," said a twenty-seven-year-old woman in response to a survey question.

Another young woman said that the most difficult thing in the world for her was to tell some guy how to kiss differently. She wanted to give her boyfriend pointers so he would kiss better, but she never did it because she simply didn't know how to tell him.

Unfortunately, we live in a society that generally discourages talking about sexual matters. Other cultures, such as natives of certain South Sea islands, including the Trobriands, are much more comfortable talking about things like kissing. Studies show, however, that both men and women like people who occasionally talk about sex. And after you read this book, you'll have plenty to talk about! Talking about kissing can be a fun and sexy thing to do. And you'll be surprised at how quickly *talking* about kissing can lead to doing it.

Probably the most important reason to talk about kissing is that even though you're compatible in every other way, you and your partner may have different views about how to kiss. One young woman said, "My boyfriend doesn't like ear kisses; he says they tickle too much. As a result, he doesn't think I'll like them either, which is dead wrong. They really turn me on!" Her complaint is a common one—many lovers have kissing preferences that their partner doesn't know about. When I asked whether people had different views about kissing from their partner, about 70 percent said yes. Many women reported that they liked to kiss more than their lover. Said one twenty-six-year-old: "I definitely like to kiss more than my husband does. I wish he got into it more." So, remember, *always ask what your partner likes*—it may be totally different from what you think.

♥ ♥ ♥

"We've read enough!" I can hear some readers clamoring.
"We're ready to close the book and kiss!"

And indeed you are, since you've been prepared by thousands of people who have told you what they like about kissing, how they do it, and what it means to them. You know more about the subject than an army of lovers. You're ready to kiss! Find your boyfriend, girlfriend, sweetheart, your soul mate, your honey, your sugar pie, your darling and pucker up! And when your lover gasps in delight and breaks off from a passionate embrace demanding that you admit where you learned to kiss like the gods of love themselves, merely contain your chuckle of triumph, smile to yourself, candidly point to your copy of this book, and prepare to revel in the sensual pleasures that belong to all who have mastered the art of kissing.

$\mathcal{I}$NDEX

Page numbers in **bold** type indicate primary references.